ONE HUNDRED YEARS OF
ARCHITECTURAL EDUCATION

1908 - 2008

GEORGIA TECH

Editors

Elizabeth Meredith Dowling

Lisa M. Thomason

Unless otherwise noted, images are part of Georgia Tech Library's archival
collection and digital repository, SMARTech; or from the personal collections
of faculty members used with their permission.

Published by:
Georgia Tech College of Architecture
247 Fourth Street NW
Atlanta, GA 30332

To order or for more information, contact the College of Architecture
Dean's Office at 404.894.3880 or e-mail coa@gatech.edu.
Also visit the College of Architecture online at http://www.coa.gatech.edu.

Concept by Alan Balfour
Project Director: Teresa A. Nagel
Copyeditor: Leslie N. Sharp

Printed by Tucker Castleberry on Lustro Offset Environmental Dull Cream Text,
FSC Certified, ECF Certified, acid free

ISBN # 978-0-9823171-0-5
2009922790

Printed in the USA, First Edition

This is a marvelous document. A complex and profound visual record, not only of the education of the architect at Georgia Tech, but a record of a society and a culture through a century of profound change.

There is pleasure in the many years of watercolor drawings; architects called them render-ings—extracting the essence. There is pleasure until the ability to paint in watercolor faded slowly over the years, and the objects being rendered became slowly less picturesque, more objective, less charming, more instrumental. Was this carried into external reality?

Look beyond changing techniques of representation to the subject matter—one hundred years of studio projects, one hundred years of exploring the object of desire. At the heart of all the forces that surround the creation of architecture—physical, financial, legal—are fic-tions. Call them visions, call it style, but they are fictions from which future realities emerge; fictions which in some intangible way satisfy the desire of a client—singular or plural, corporate or public.

Look closely at these ten decades of shifting, staged fictions—what plays do they anticipate? Look closely at how the people, the actors, are portrayed.

Observe the first thirty years of the gentlemen architect providing service to his social equals. See the project modernism (in which Georgia Tech was as progressive as any in the nation), beginning as merely a style and then becoming increasingly committed to the politics of social change.

Observe the widening of horizons as the architects' visions soar above the above and beyond … French-inspired monuments, through German order, into the brave austerity and idealism of the post-war years, into the sixties and the acceptance of the dreams of women, then, into the increasingly giddy seventies and eighties, some decades much more confident than others.

Trace in the work faltering visions and uncertainty; a waning confidence in opposing the status quo. See the first signs of a return to tangible and familiar words—a concern for a con-tinuity of style, a pleasure in building traditions, and the emergence, for the first time since the forties, of a tolerance for, and engagement with, a reality of pluralism.

See in what follows a feast of evidence in which each of us, from our own experiences, can find revealing insights into the dreams and aspirations that shaped not just Atlanta and the South, but the Nation in the last century.

— Alan Balfour
Dean and Professor
College of Architecture, Georgia Tech

TABLE OF CONTENTS

PREFACE

Georgia Tech figures into my earliest childhood memories because mine was a Georgia Tech family—my father Bill, ME 1934, my brother Bill, IM 1962, and me, B ARCH 1971. I imagine I am not the only offspring of a loyal alumnus who listened at the Sunday dinner table to the heroic stories of George Griffin delivered with far more enthusiasm and color than those retellings of true family events. My father was a member of the Yellow Jacket Club and later as an alumnus of the White and Gold Club. When I was college-aged, he gave me a copy of *Dress Her in White and Gold* and, to the great horror of my brother, sent me off to be one of the few women students at Georgia Tech in the 1960s. Even though I have been closely associated with Georgia Tech through my education and more than thirty years of teaching architectural history, much was learned in the research for this centennial celebration; and I now have a greater understanding of Georgia Tech and its blossoming into an internationally respected institution. I had the good fortune to count P. M. Heffernan, James H. Grady, Frank Beckum, and Joe Smith as friends, but understanding the significant ways that they affected the school only took shape with this project.

In 2003, I approached the late Dean Thomas Tom Galloway (1939-2007) with an armload of centennial books from other architecture schools and a proposal to write a detailed history of our Architecture Program. As we remember, he saw his position as head of all programs and did not believe in singling out one for such a major retrospective. Two years later, I persisted with a reduced agenda of a display of the history and student work through the one hundred years. He agreed to support this idea and thus began research lasting from 2005 to 2009. My co-editor Lisa Thomason learned of the project in the fall of 2005 while a student in my elective class on American classicism. Her research for the course included a study of the Beaux-Arts Institute of Design and the published examples of Georgia Tech student work. I had given this same assignment many times in the past, but Lisa became intrigued with the work and asked to continue the research. Thus began an academic hunt to recover the history of the Architecture Program. Lisa became a well-known figure in the Georgia Tech Library Archives who plumbed the depths of information available in yearly reports, *Blueprints, Techniques*, and various newspaper clippings.

The collection of student work that makes this book possible survives somewhat by chance. For most of its life, the drawings were housed in flat files in the morgue—a storage and mechanical room prone to flooding on the second floor of the old architecture building. Where the drawings were housed from the 1920s when the collection begins until the 1950s when the Architecture Building was built is not known. Prior to 1924, student work had been published in yearly annuals and then afterward every other year until 1931. After this date, the publication ceases, but the collection of retained work began in earnest in 1926. Until 1986, professors regularly retained student work—design projects, life drawings, analysis studies—sufficient to understand instruction from an era. In total, 1,518 items are now housed in the Georgia Tech Library Archives. After 1986, examples survived in the personal collections of individual professors—especially Richard Dagenhart. The process of systematically retaining digital images of student work has recently begun.

This book and the three exhibits prominently displayed over the course of the 2008-2009 school year were the inspiration of Dean Alan Balfour, who joined the college in July 2008. With his encouragement, the previously envisioned simple library exhibit took on a new life, allowing this presentation of the remarkable talent of one hundred years of architectural education at Georgia Tech.

— Elizabeth Meredith Dowling

ACKNOWLEDGEMENTS

Both the exhibit and this book documenting the one hundred years of architectural education at Georgia Tech depended on the generous efforts of many individuals and organizations. We would like to extend special thanks to Cathy Carpenter for allowing the Architecture Library to be the staging ground for the exhibit production and for enthusiastically assisting in the use of the library as a gallery space, thus allowing the display of original material; to Leslie Sharp for hours devoted to editing all manuscripts and sharpening the focus of the writing; to Teri Nagel for maintaining the highest quality of production in the face of extreme financial conditions; to Richard Dagenhart for retaining examples of student work; to Lane Duncan for organizing the watercolor display; to Doug Allen for providing continuity in support of the project following the unexpected passing of Dean Tom Galloway; to Alan Balfour for bringing an expanded vision to the meaning of the centennial; to Chris Dierks and the Van Alen Institute for giving early access to the BAID work of Georgia Tech students in the midst of their own production schedule; to Jody Thompson, Kirk Henderson, and Mandi Johnson of the Georgia Tech Library Archives for assistance in displays and access to all material used in the exhibit; to Becky Fitzgibbon for help in mounting the exhibit; to the College's Information Technology staff for printing the exhibits and solving innumerable problems; to Georgia Tech Communications and Marketing for their technical assistance; to the College of Architecture Alumni Committee for their financial support; and to countless students who assisted in small and large ways to achieve the celebration of a lifetime.

Additional thanks to:
College of Architecture Faculty
Ellen Dunham-Jones, Associate Professor and Director of Architecture Program; Lars Spuybroek, Professor and Thomas W. Ventulett, III Chair in Architectural Design; David Green, Professor of Practice; Robert M. Craig, Professor; Mark Cottle, Associate Professor; Richard Dagenhart, Associate Professor; Harris Dimitropoulos, Associate Professor; Athanassios Economou, Associate Professor; Michael Gamble, Associate Professor; George B. Johnston, Associate Professor; Sabir Khan, Associate Professor and Associate Dean; W. Jude Leblanc, Associate Professor; Charles Rudolph, Associate Professor; Gernot Riether, Assistant Professor; Frances Hsu, Assistant Professor; Franca Trubiano, Assistant Professor; Tristan Al-Haddad, Visiting Assistant Professor; Daniel Baerlecken, Visiting Assistant Professor; Frederick Pearsall, Senior Lecturer; Jonathan Lacrosse, Part-time Lecturer; Ann Gerondelis, Common First Year Coordinator

College of Architecture Information Technology Staff
Robert Gerhart Jr., Director, Support Services; Trent Chima, Department Manager; Perry Minyard, Systems Support Specialist III; Paul Cook, Systems Support Specialist II; Jeff Langston, Computer Services Specialist; Ieva Mikolaviciute, Student Assistant; Ariel Wu, Student Assistant

Georgia Tech Price Gilbert Memorial Library Scholarly Communications and Digital Services Department
Sara Fuchs, Repository Manager; Kathryn Gentilello, Digital Projects Coordinator; Julie Speer, Head, Scholarly Communications and Digital Initiatives

IMAGINE Lab
Anatoliusz "Tolek" Lesniewski, Director; Jonathan Shaw, Research Scientist II; Matthew Swarts, Research Scientist I; Erik Palmquist, Research Scientist I; Graceline "Racel" Williams, Research Scientist I

College of Architecture Students
Undergraduate students Leeland McPhail, Laura Richter; Tiffany Savage, BS ARCH 2008
M ARCH Candidates Merica May Jensen, Josef Fischer, Reginald Tabor, David Pearson, Paul Knight, Ian Lauer, Jonathan Aprati, David Biel, Matt Erwin, Tristan Hall, Arseni Zaitsev, BS ARCH 2006, GTA Lecturer

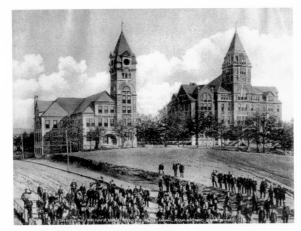

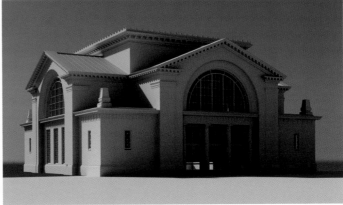

CLOCKWISE FROM TOP LEFT: Shop Building and Administration Building, Georgia School of Technology, c.1888; Forge room in the Shop Building, c.1909; *Archeology Project*, R. C. Dean, Second Medal, published in *BAID Bulletin*, May 1928 (courtesy of Van Alen Institute's Design Competitions Archive); *A Ferry Terminal for New York City*, Tim Kelly, MS ARCH 2008, computer rendering, 2007, for Master of Science program in architecture with an emphasis on classical design; *Analytique*, H.W. Phillips, First Mention, published in *BAID Bulletin*, August 1930 (courtesy of Van Alen Institute's Design Competitions Archive)

Founding Principles:
Continuing Influence of the Beaux-Arts on Architectural Education

Elizabeth Meredith Dowling

In 1885, the Georgia School of Technology received official authorization from the state legislature, but did not begin instruction until 1888. During the interim, construction of the first two campus buildings projected the equality of the "hand-mind" philosophy of the new technological training. Designed by the firm of Bruce and Morgan, the Shop Building (the "hand") and the Administration Building (the "mind") displayed similar prominent towers like many of the collegiate buildings the firm would design for Agnes Scott College, Clemson University, and Auburn University. Of these two original campus buildings, the superior status held by the one representing the "mind" over that of the "hand" was subtly indicated by the greater mass of the Administration Building, which contained lecture rooms, chemical laboratory, a library, mechanical drawing rooms, a chapel, and offices. Engineering schools of the era combined scientific studies with physical hands-on shop work where students produced saleable goods to provide financial support for their school. Georgia Tech would follow such a shop culture that elevated the status of physical labor alongside traditional academic courses. A woodworking department, machine shop, forge room, and foundry existed in the Shop Building, with the latter causing the fire that significantly damaged the building within the first decade of its existence. Items produced by the students included bookends, doorstops, and gates for mausoleums at Atlanta's Oakland Cemetery. At our founding, the derogatory reference to the "North Avenue Trade School" was fitting.

Although the authority to establish an architecture program was included in the initial bill creating the technological school, the only academic major offered was in mechanical engineering, and this would remain until 1897 when majors in electrical and civil engineering were added to the degree offerings. Although an architecture curriculum did not arrive at Georgia Tech for two decades, the idea of improving the quality of architects and architecture in Georgia was promoted in the meantime. Both A.C. Bruce and Thomas H. Morgan, both of whom received their architectural training in the apprenticeship system, promoted the professionalization of architecture through higher education. In an article published in 1890, Morgan wrote that:

> . . .the State University should provide a department of architecture presided over by an architect of known training in art, and skilled in construction. This field will then be open to the student. It is a profession with possibilities for greatness with requirements in skilled training second to none, and the systematic study of architecture in the State University would soon be seen in the better and most artistic character of our buildings.[1]

When our Architectural Program finally began in 1908, a tradition of training architects was more typical in the academic offerings of major universities. Formal architectural education had emerged in the United States in 1865 with the founding of Boston Tech, which was later renamed the Massachusetts Institute of Technology. By 1900, programs in architecture had also been established at Cornell University, University of Illinois, Syracuse University, University of Michigan, Columbia University, University of Pennsylvania, Columbian College (now George Washington University), Armour Institute (now Illinois Institute of Technology), and Harvard University. Architectural education did not reach Southern colleges until 1907 when the first program in the region was founded at Alabama Polytechnic Institute, later renamed Auburn University. The following year, our program and one at Tulane University were founded.[2]

All of these programs ultimately shared a common lineage—the Ecole des Beaux-Arts in Paris. Established in 1671 during the reign of Louis XIV, the French Académie Royale d'Architecture and its associated school was not the first of its kind, but it was the longest continuously developed mode of architectural education in the West, surviving until the student upheavals of 1968. In 1846, Richard Morris Hunt, the well-known architect of the Vanderbilt mansions and the Metropolitan Museum of Art, matriculated at the Ecole, which made him the first American to pursue formal academic training in architecture. Later after establishing his office in New York City, he opened the first atelier to train his own employees in the design skills he had acquired in Paris. One of his students, William Ware, would later go on to translate this knowledge into the academic program of Massachusetts Institute of Technology's architecture curriculum—the first such program in America. Our nation's colleges maintained a close association with the Ecole by hiring French studio critics, and as will be discussed later, by providing students the opportunity to study in Paris.

Intellectually the most profound influence on American education was the French critic who arrived in his new home ready to share the sophisticated culture, traditions and architectural knowledge of Parisian life. Although we did not have a French critic on our faculty, through the decades we were closely associated with France. By far the most well known of these French critics was Paul Cret, who was hired by the University of Pennsylvania in 1903 and continued teaching there until 1937. Cret's lasting influence on American architecture cannot be overstated. Not only did he produce many fine buildings around the country, but he also taught hundreds of future architects. One of the best known today would be Louis Kahn. But of greater significance to Georgia Tech was a student from Cret's earliest years, our first long-term director of Architecture, Francis Palmer Smith.

The actual initiation of the Architecture Program at Georgia Tech does not owe its start to the thoughtful deliberation of the college administration, but instead to an enthusiastic twenty-year old civil engineering student named Earnest Daniel "Ed" Ivey (1887-1966). In 1907, Ed Ivey met with Georgia Tech President Kenneth G. Matheson (1864-1931) to discuss the creation of an architecture program. But rather than actively supporting a new curriculum in architecture, Matheson placed upon Ivey the burden of finding a group of students interested in the subject. Ivey succeeded in finding twenty students who wanted to pursue this educational direction and the program was initiated in 1908. The first curriculum of the program emphasized the visual with classes in architectural drawing, descriptive geometry, elements of architecture, shades and shadows, and perspective—and this was just in the freshman year. More advanced classes were offered in freehand drawing, pen and ink rendering, and watercolor drawing. These artistic skills were balanced with courses in theoretical knowledge drawn from the history of architecture, historic ornament, archeology, and the history of painting. The practical side of architectural studies began in the freshman year with a full year of shop work followed in the sophomore and junior years with courses in building construction, sanitation, structural mechanics, and professional practice. In the sophomore through senior years, a single study termed "design" was listed.

In 1909, Francis Palmer Smith joined the Georgia Tech faculty fresh from his studies with his professor Paul Cret at the University of Pennsylvania. The character drawn from the Ecole-Penn connection remained with the program for the following decades. The concept of studio instruction, the types of projects offered, and the rendering techniques employed reflected an Americanized version of the Ecole approach. As in the French system, students began with small, less complicated building types and proceeded to those of greater complexity through the four years of their education. Projects were presented in one of two ways—an analytique or a rendered project. The analytique, often named an archeology, was a study-method of dissecting a building and presenting it as a single-board composition. The lessons learned included details, scale, proportion, composition, and rendering. This knowledge assisted in the design of full buildings and even in the arrangement of a working drawing sheet that followed the same compositional logic learned through the analytique. The single-board presentation would include elevation, horizontal and vertical sections, and large scale details.

The rendered project always began with an *esquisse*. The *esquisse* could be the end product and, if this was the case, it was usually named an *esquisse-esquisse*. The *esquisse* was created in twelve to twenty-four hours. The essential plan conception was thus established that would be developed in sections and elevations over the subsequent weeks. The value of this system was moving the student's efforts beyond the all-consuming search for the ideal plan, which is still so often the greatest pitfall today. Cret defended this method against modernist detractors by pointing out that a studio project is after all only a method of learning and that there was as much to be learned in developing a bad plan as in spending an entire project searching for a perfect plan. With the concept set by an *esquisse*, the student could spend the full six or eight weeks exploring elevations, interiors, materials, and details.

From as early as 1911, our school had formed a relationship with the Beaux-Arts Institute of Design (BAID) in New York. This organization was established by men who had attended the Ecole and were devoted to improving the quality of American architecture. Their method was simple—the organization produced design programs that could be adopted for use in schools around the country. The most impressive work in a college studio or a private atelier was sent to New York for judging, and the best of these projects were given awards and were published in the *BAID Bulletin*. The concept survived from 1904 to 1956, and the process allowed visual comparison and juried competition between students in far-flung state schools and those in established, well-funded private universities. The value for a small public school in the South was immense. Georgia Tech had an established record of consistent remarkable success. In 1939, a grand fete was held in Brittain Dining Hall to receive the BAID prize for Georgia Tech architectural students having won the greatest number of prize-winning projects for the year. The New York architect John Mead Howells, co-designer of the Chicago Tribune Tower, gave the award. Through the years, the BAID name and funding changed, but the offering of competition prizes remained constant. The most widely recognized competitions administered by the foundation and its successors were the Lloyd Warren Fellowship - Paris Prize in Architecture and then later the Van Alen Prize. For each of these, many Georgia Tech students either won or placed with great frequency as is documented in this book.

Although student work over the one hundred years in the Architecture Program changed in appearance reflecting the prevailing stylistic trends, the organization and many of the fundamental design principles have remained constant. Programs are issued, design instruction occurs in the studio over a period of weeks, concepts are created and developed, solutions are organized into formal presentations, and finally a jury of knowledgeable critics offers their opinions of the work. Over time the popularity of various presentation media changes, but the love of evocative drawings is always evident. The greatest potential change is associated with the introduction of the computer to the studio, but digital rendering is unrelated to style or period; it is merely another useful tool, that is as long as it does not limit creative thought. The current eclecticism of our program today at the College of Architecture reflects the diversity of worldwide architectural practice. The reemergence of design that promotes the development of traditional skills, such as hand sketching and rendering in pencil, ink, and watercolor, alongside the study of proportion and detailing, demonstrates that powerful design concepts continue to have relevance for clients in the twenty-first century. The desire to create beautiful, aesthetically pleasing buildings was the focus of the early decades of our Architecture Program's instruction and continues as such today.

—Elizabeth M. Dowling, PhD, is a Professor of Architecture at Georgia Tech.

NOTES

1. Warren E. Drury III, "The Architectural Development of Georgia Tech: A Thesis" (Master's Thesis, Georgia Institute of Technology, 1984), 47; Editorial Notes, *Southern Architect and Building News* (June 1980), vol. 1, no. 8, 107.

2. Arthur Clason Weatherhead and James Philip Noffsinger have slightly different information on the first schools founded. Arthur Clason Weatherhead, *The History of Collegiate Education in Architecture in the United States: A Dissertation* (Columbia University, 1941), 235-237; James Philip Noffsinger, *The Influence of the Ecole des Beaux-arts on the Architects of the United States: A Dissertation* (The Catholic University of America: Washington, D.C., 1955).

LEFT: P. H. Clark, *A City Bank*, Sophomore Design, 1911-1912
ABOVE: F. L. Rand, *Freshman Rendering*, 1911-1912

LAUNCHING ARCHITECTURAL EDUCATION: 1908 - 1912

The history of the Architecture Program begins in 1907 with a meeting initiated by Ernest Daniel "Ed" Ivey (1887-1966), a civil engineering major, with President Matheson to discuss the creation of a Department of Architecture. Matheson identified architecture as "essentially a Fine Art," and the course curriculum included the history of architecture and the "work of construction in practical form." In September 1908, the first courses in architecture at Georgia Tech were offered. In 1911, Ivey left Tech before receiving a degree to begin his career in architecture, but he was considered an honorary alumnus by the Department of Architecture. Also in that year, the first Bachelor of Science in Architecture degrees were granted to I. M. Auld, W. P. Barney, R. A. Burroughs, J. T. Clarke, J. E. Crane, M. H. Levy, and W. A. Markley. These graduates placed Georgia Tech among the first public universities in the United States to offer an architecture degree. By 1912, the Department of Architecture had grown to forty-two full-time students and three faculty members.

Course of Study in Architecture, 1908

Freshman Year
Mathematics, English, Chemistry, Shop Work, Physical Culture, Architectural Drawing, Descriptive Geometry,
Elements of Architecture, Shades and Shadows, Perspective

Sophomore Year
Mathematics, English, Physics, Building Construction, Elements of Architecture, Design, History of Architecture, Freehand Drawing

Junior Year
English, French, Building Construction, Sanitation, Graphic Statics, Structural Mechanics, Design, History of Architecture,
Historic Ornament, Pen and Ink Rendering, Freehand Drawing, Watercolor Drawing

Senior Year
French, Professional Practice, Special Lectures, History of Painting, Archaeology, Freehand Drawing, Pen and Ink Rendering,
Watercolor Drawing, Design

James M. Russell, *A Niche in a Garden Wall*, Sophomore Analytique Design, 1911-1912

TOP LEFT: In 1912, Philip Trammell Shutze (1890-1982) received a Bachelor of Science in Architecture, graduating cum laude. Shutze, who went on to become one of the program's most prominent alumni, was hired the same year as a professor of architecture and also worked as the designer in the firm of Hentz, Reid, and Adler. In 1915, he won the Rome Prize Fellowship, which included residence in Rome and travel in Europe for three years with all expenses paid by the American Academy in Rome. "Alas, he drew so much one day / He failed to draw his breath." (Shutze in the 1912 *Blueprint*)

TOP RIGHT: Faculty of the Georgia School of Technology, 1908
President Kenneth G. Matheson (1864-1931), third from left, bottom row

BOTTOM LEFT: Seven students of the original twenty graduated from the Department of Architecture in 1911, followed by four more students in 1912: D. A. Finlayson, F. H. Ogletree, P. T. Shutze, and H. D. Stubbs.

BOTTOM RIGHT: Francis Palmer Smith (1886-1971) received a Bachelor of Science in Architecture from the University of Pennsylvania in 1907. He then served as a professor and first head of the newly founded Department of Architecture at the Georgia School of Technology. He served in this position from 1909 to 1922, when he left to form the highly productive architecture firm of Pringle and Smith.

TOP: F. H. Ogletree, The Tomb of a National Hero, Mention, BAID, Senior Design, 1911-1912
BOTTOM LEFT: Philip T. Shutze, *A Monumental Staircase*, Senior Design 1911-1912
BOTTOM RIGHT: Philip T. Shutze, *The Central Pavillion of an Art Museum*, Second Mention, BAID, Junior Design, 1911-1912

M. C. Kollack, Jr., Untitled Watercolor, 1915-1916

R. A. Preas, *Facade of a Public Building*, 1915-1916

EARLY PROGRESS: 1912 - 1916

During these years, the program began hiring more faculty. A notable example was James Herbert "Doc" Gailey, a professor of architecture in 1912, who received his Bachelor of Architecture and Master of Architecture degrees from the University of Pennsylvania. Gailey became a renowned architect of the Atlanta area while teaching architecture courses at Georgia Tech. He became the first Professor Emeritus in the Department of Architecture, with forty-two years of service. Many of the earlier directors and professors in the Department had matriculated at Harvard University and University of Pennsylvania, two of the oldest schools of architecture in the United States.

The Department of Architecture occupied the third floor of the Electrical Building (opposite, bottom left) from 1908 to 1920. The area was divided into drafting rooms, studio, lecture room, and an office.

Philanthropist Andrew Carnegie donated funds for the construction of Georgia Tech's first library (opposite, bottom right), completed in 1907. Housed within this Carnegie Library, the Architecture Library (now located in the West Architecture Building) included collections of books, photographs, drawings, stereopticon slides, and plaster casts.

E. M. Jackson, *A Historical Society Building*, Mention, BAID, Junior Design, 1915-1916

W. C. Holleyman, *A Central Feature of a Museum*, 1915-1916

CLUBS AND SOCIETIES

During the 1915-1916 academic year, when just fifty students were enrolled in the Department of Architecture, they had already formed various small clubs and societies to share their common interests in art and architecture and to promote the development of the Architecture Program. At the time, social clubs centered on academic fields were virtually unheard of on the Georgia Tech campus.

OPPOSITE LEFT: I. M. Auld, W. P. Barney, E. D. Ivey, P. T. Shutze, and J. T. Clarke, students in the Department of Architecture, founded the Artist Club in 1910. This club was organized to promote the fine arts of sculpture, drawing, painting, and architecture. Their tongue-in-cheek motto was: "Art for the model's sake, Architecture for the money's sake."

OPPOSITE RIGHT: Students of the Department of Architecture founded the Architectural Society in 1910 to "promote the interests of the Architectural Department of Tech." The first officers were E. D. Ivey as president, P. T. Shutze as vice president, R. A. Burroughs as treasurer, and W. E. Irvin as secretary.

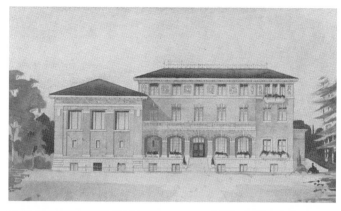

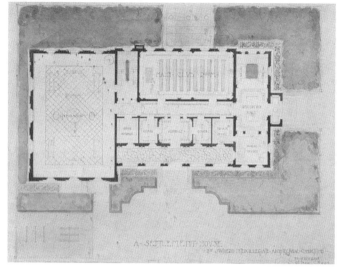

T. H. Henderson, *A Settlement House,* Junior Design, First Prize
Southern Intercollegiate Competition, 1915-1916

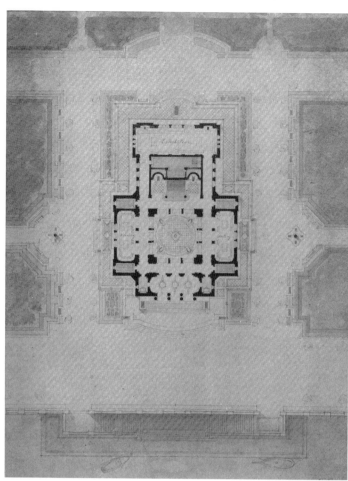

M. C. Kollack, Jr., *A Government Exposition Building,* Senior Design, 1915-1916

Flippen D. Burge
A Metropolitan Church
Senior Design, 1916

Burge and Stevens Architects and Engineers
James R. Wilkinson, Associate
Apartment Project for Georgia Tech
Renderings for *Callaway Apartments* (top) and
Flippen D. Burge Apartments (bottom)
Gouache on Board, 1956

EXPANDED CURRICULUM AND A NEW DIRECTOR

In 1920, the Department of Architecture offered two educational paths: a regular course of four years leading to the Bachelor of Science in Architecture degree and a two-year Special Course, open to qualified draftsmen with three or more years experience in the office of a practicing architect, leading to a Certificate of Proficiency. The Special Course implemented two years of purely architectural courses in drawing, design, and construction, supplemented with classes in Mechanical Plant and English, taken in the Evening School of Applied Sciences.

This particular program was meant originally for the practicing architect to gain more knowledge and continue their education in architecture. Architectural drafting courses were given for a two-year degree, also ending in a Certificate of Proficiency. Students who have not worked in the field, but attended night classes for Architectural Drafting, had the option of taking an additional three years of regular architectural undergraduate coursework in the Department of Architecture to receive the Certificate of Proficiency appropriate for practice.

LEFT: In 1922, John Llewelyn Skinner, who received a Master of Architecture from Harvard in 1921, was named director of the Department of Architecture and held this position until 1925, at which time he left to start an architecture program at the University of Miami.

MIDDLE: In 1920, the Department of Architecture moved from the third floor of the Electrical Building to the third floor of the Mechanical Engineering Building.

RIGHT: In 1922, the Department of Architecture moved from the Mechanical Engineering Building to the Physics Building, where it remained until 1952.

Samuel G. Stoney, Jr., *An Entrance to a Museum*
Sophomore Design, 1920

George H. Gibson, *A College Hall*
Second Prize, Seventh Southern
Intercollegiate Competition
Sophomore Design, 1919-1920

William H. Merriam, *A College Dormitory*
Sophomore Design, 1920

TERMINOLOGY

ANALYTIQUE. An analysis drawing incorporating plan, section, elevation, perspective, and details into a drawing judged on the beauty and clarity of its composition. The study could either represent a historic building or a new design analysis.

BEAUX-ARTS INSTITUTE OF DESIGN (BAID). A national organization founded in 1916 dedicated to the improvement of architectural education by providing a centralized location for the distribution and judging of design problems. Schools throughout the United States sent student work to New York to be judged and their resulting publication allowed comparison of the quality of design work on a nationwide basis. In 1956, the name changed to National Institute for Architectural Education and in 1996 was renamed the Van Alen Institute after its endowment by the designer of the Chrysler Building.

CLASS A. Upper-level project equivalent to *première classe* of the Ecole des Beaux-Arts.

CLASS B. Lower-level project equivalent to *seconde classe* of the Ecole des Beaux-Arts.

ESQUISSE. A twelve to twenty-four hour project that results in a partial schematic design that was either the final assignment or the initial design for a more lengthy project.

LIFE DRAWING. Sketching live models was an essential part of the architecture curriculum. At the Ecole in Paris, students learned to draw by first redrawing sketches of accepted masters, next drawing from plaster casts, and finally moving to the more complex rendition of live models.

LLOYD WARREN FELLOWSHIP - PARIS PRIZE IN ARCHITECTURE. Brothers Lloyd and Whitney Warren devoted great energy to the improvement of architectural education in the United States. Whitney Warren along with Thomas Hastings and Ernest Flagg established the Society of Beaux-Arts Architects in 1894. From this organization, Lloyd Warren incorporated the Beaux-Arts Institute of Design. The brothers funded the Warren Prize given to the best student planning solution each year. Lloyd Warren along with numerous distinguished Americans founded the Paris Prize in 1903. In 1904, he obtained permission from the French government allowing the prize winner to enter the first class level of the Ecole des Beaux-Arts. After Lloyd Warren's accidental death, permanent funds were raised by 1926 to continue the prize in his memory. In the early years, the prize offered a two and a half year fellowship at the Ecole. The length of time abroad has gradually diminished and, at present, is principally a traveling scholarship.

MENTION AND MEDALS. Terms derived from French grading system.

OPPOSITE:

TOP LEFT: Roy E. Hitchcock, *San Pietro*, Analytique, 1939

TOP RIGHT: E. M. Jackson, *A Bank Screen*, Nine-Hour Sketch, 1915-1916

BOTTOM LEFT: William Halbert Barnett, Esquisse, 1938

BOTTOM RIGHT: M. T. Dawson, *A Romanesque Portal*, Archeology, 1923

C. Dubose, *The Minis House,* Archeology, BAID Second Medal, 1928
Courtesy of Van Alen Institute's Design Competitions Archive

H. E. Edwards, Analytique, 1934
Courtesy of Van Alen Institute's Design Competitions Archive

Architecture courses of this period were often organized around a series of competitive projects ranging from esquisse to analytique to more complex Class A projects, with juried awards all supervised by the Beaux-Arts Institute of Design (BAID). The Department of Architecture focused the final project of the year on submission for the annual Lloyd Warren Fellowship-Paris Prize competition, which supported the winner for study abroad of two-and-a-half years at the Ecole des Beaux-Arts.

The prestigious Paris Prize national design competition (created in 1904), encouraged submissions of complex Class A projects from students and professional architects. Another distinguished juried award sponsored by the Southern Intercollegiate Competition was a popular student competition, and a top-place honor would bring the recipient national recognition. Beginning in 1922, students of the Department of Architecture placed first and second in the Southern Intercollegiate Competition for five years in a row, and seniors in design had received Mentions in numerous BAID competitions in New York.

C. Dubose, *A Summer Residence for the Mayor of a Metropolis*
Class A Project, BAID, 1928
Courtesy of Van Alen Institute's Design Competitions Archive

H. McD. Martin, Class A Project, BAID Second Medal, 1928
Courtesy of Van Alen Institute's Design Competitions Archive

Despite the changes in instructional methodology over the first half of the twentieth century, the concept of teaching design through participation in competitions has prevailed. Over the years, student entries in several key regional and national architectural competitions helped instill in students an ability to exercise creativity within the framework of sound design technique. Further, these competitions brought students to the attention of the broader architectural community, and their success reflected well on Georgia Tech.

Whether representative of the classical order of the Beaux-Arts system or the more industrial approach of the Bauhaus, it is the understanding of the hierarchy of forms, the conceptual arrangement not lost in detail, and the theory of architecture in space, people, and structures alike that validates the art of architecture.

William H. Kwilecki, *An Infirmary for a Private School*
Senior Design, BAID, 1915-1916

The Southern Intercollegiate Architectural Competition, for example, was first held in the fall 1913 for the Intercollegiate Problem in Design, specifically for senior classes of architecture from accredited Southern, Western, and Eastern universities in the United States. That year, seventeen student designs were submitted and judged by members of the architectural faculty of the University of Pennsylvania. Three of five designs submitted by Georgia Tech architecture students were awarded Equal First Place (W. E. Conklin, W. E. Dunwoody, Fred L. Rand) and one other received a Mention (M.W. Lott). Between 1913 and 1923, Georgia Tech architecture students received nine First Prizes, five Second Prizes, and thirteen Mentions, which reflected well on the Department of Architecture.

Frank W. Manning, *The Court of Honor of a University*
Third Mention, Tenth Southern Intercollegiate Competition, Junior Design, 1922-1923

The Architectural Arts League of Atlanta awarded two annual prize memberships in its organization to those members of the senior class in architecture having the highest general grade point average during the first three years in the program. Awards were made in October of each year and covered payment of all membership dues while at Georgia Tech. In 1910, the awards were given to F.H. Ogletree, BS ARCH 1911, and P.T. Shutze, BS ARCH 1912.

The American Institute of Architects awarded annually The School Medal and a copy of Henry Adams' *Mont St. Michel and Chartres* to the most promising senior in each accredited architecture school. Hugh Stubbins, BS ARCH 1933, James L. Skinner, BS ARCH 1935, and James Finch, BS ARCH 1936, were some recipients of this award.

The Architectural Alumni Prize awarded a set of architectural books to the senior architecture student who had submitted the best design in one of the "regular" problems. In 1913, F. L. Rand was the recipient of this prize.

ABOVE: Henry David Anastasas, *A Mosaic Pavement/Late Romanesque/Early Renaissance*, Ink, Watercolor on White Paper, 34.5 x 52 inches Junior Design, 1928

LEFT: Lee C. McClure, *A Romanesque Portal*, Archeology Junior Design 1922-1923

In 1925, the Department received the distinction of being the first school in the South to be elected to the Association of Collegiate Schools of Architecture (ACSA), consisting of only the most respected architectural schools in the country. The same year, the American Institute of Architects designated it as an accredited school. In 1927, the Department of Architecture at Georgia School of Technology was the largest in the South, having over one hundred students and seven faculty members.

Sanford Ayers, *Jewish Synagogue*
Senior Design, 1926

Walter Harmon Aldred
Pencil, Watercolor on Board, 42 x 30 inches
Senior Design, 1927

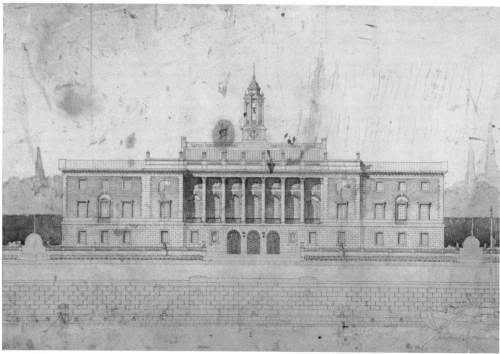

The then-President Marion Brittain's efforts to improve the curriculum in the 1920s and the earlier inclusion of the Department of Architecture into the existing strictly technical Institute curriculum in 1908, with its notable achievements along the way, helped lead Georgia Tech to becoming a member of the Southern Association of Colleges and Secondary Schools in 1925, the only Southern school to be admitted at the time. As historians August Giebelhaus and Robert McMath noted, "With the broadening of the school's curriculum to include a degree that combined applied art as well as technical skill, the Georgia School of Technology stepped outside the niche it occupied as a first rate technical school 'second to none in the work it undertakes to do' to take its place among the premiere academic institutions in the New South" (*Engineering the New South: Georgia Tech, 1885-1985 (1985)*, 171).

H. G. Law, *A Moorish Court with a Pool*, BAID Second Medal, Archaeology Project, 1929
Courtesy of Van Alen Institute's Design Competitions Archive

M. Atwater, *A Moorish Court with a Pool*, BAID Second Medal, Archaeology Project, 1929
Courtesy of Van Alen Institute's Design Competitions Archive

Carol M. Smith, *Entrance to a Small Exposition* (detail)
Twelve-Hour Sketch, Freshman Design, 1926

R. Swicegood, *Gothic Building*
Ink on White Paper, 32.5 x 22.5 inches, 1928

SEMINAL EVENTS AFFECTING ARCHITECTURAL EDUCATION

— The Bauhaus School was founded by Walter Gropius in Weimar, Germany, in 1919.
   The Bauhaus School moved to Dessau, Germany, in 1925, then to Berlin, Germany, in 1932,
   and finally closed in 1933.
— *Chicago Tribune* competition in 1922: Among the entries were the first illustrations of
   European Modernism by Walter Gropius and Adolf Meyer
— Exposition Internationale des Arts Decoratifs et Industriels Modernes in Paris, France, in 1925,
   which provided impetus for the creation of a new ornamented modernism referred to as Art Deco
— Publishing of the English translation of Le Corbusier's book, *Towards A New Architecture* (1927)
— Death of leading American classicist Bertram Goodhue (1869-1924)
— Economic depression beginning in 1930
— America enters World War II in 1941

Howell B. Hulsey, Watercolor on Board, 51 x 41.5 inches, Senior Design, 1927

CHANGE IN LEADERSHIP

This period marked the beginning of the transition from the Beaux-Arts tradition of architectural design to a modernistic ideology inspired by the Bauhaus movement, established with ideas of functionalism and minimalism. Art Deco prefaced the coming of this ideology with streamlined designs. The Chicago Tribune tower illustrated the first examples of modern skyscrapers, whose language transformed the cityscape of modern metropolises. LeCorbusier's *Towards a New Architecture* further touched on the futuristic visions of the modern city. Although a different aesthetic was introduced, the foundation of Beaux-Arts studio instruction remained.

Architecture Department Head James L. Skinner resigned his position in 1925 to practice architecture in Miami, Florida. His replacement, Harold Bush-Brown, shifted the focus of instruction from the Beaux-Arts vocabulary of detail, proportions, and influence of the past towards the Bauhaus influence of theory and abstraction. He brought in many faculty who were alumni of the Harvard Graduate School of Design and who had studied under modernist Walter Gropius. Among them were D.J. "Jim" Edwards, Thomas Godfrey, and Samuel T. Hurst. They brought an interesting sequence of guest lecturers and visiting design critics, all disciplined in the modern movement, such as Walter Gropius himself, Marcel Breuer, and I.M. Pei. In the post-World War I period, when enrollment was growing dramatically, these changes had an immediate impact.

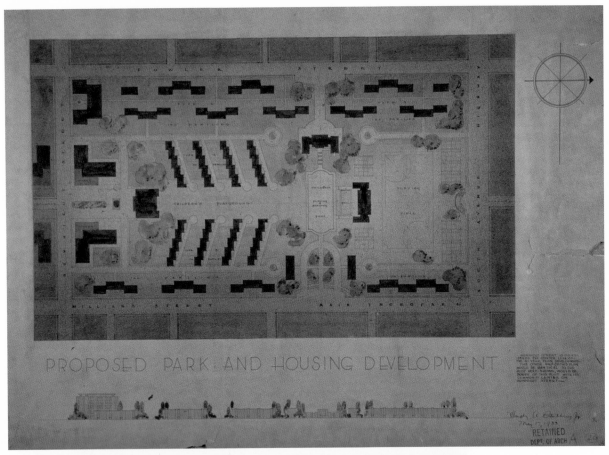

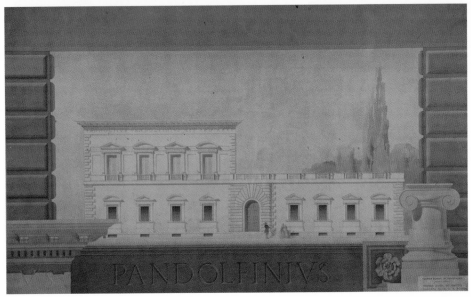

ABOVE: Hugh A. Stubbins, Jr., *Proposed Park and Housing Development*
Ink, Airbrush, Watercolor on White Paper, 39 x 28 inches
Sophomore Design, 1929

LEFT: Harry Wilborn Philips, *Pandolfini Palace*
Pencil, Watercolor on White Paper, 37 x 23 inches
Senior Design, 1932

In the 1930s, architectural education in the United States was based on two different models, the Ecole des Beaux-Arts from France and the Bauhaus from Germany. In his book *Beaux Arts to Bauhaus and Beyond: An Architect's Perspective* (1976), Harold Bush-Brown commented on the transition to the Bauhaus method of instruction: "There is no doubt that the two systems, that of the Beaux Arts and that of the Bauhaus, were at opposite poles in their philosophy and in their teaching methods. The tradition of the Beaux Arts was the search for the ideal of formal and elaborate beauty, and this could best be encouraged by the glorification of the individual through the granting of honor awards. The Bauhaus was dedicated to producing buildings that enable maximum service, taking full advantage of what the machine has to offer in achieving simple, unpretentious but efficient results."

1835 HOLT 1931

LEFT: Oliver M. Riley, Analytique, 1933

BELOW: William B. Harelson, Class B Project, 1938

A SMALL
PUBLIC
LIBRARY

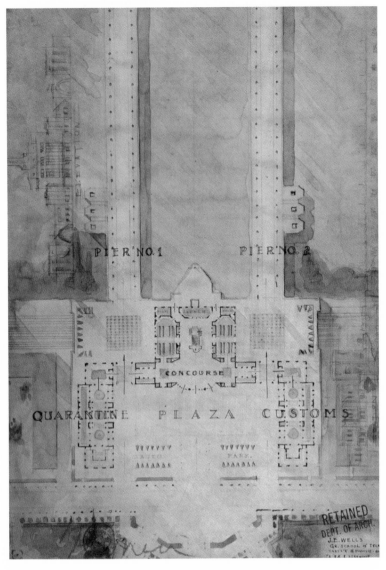

James E. Wells, *A Railroad and Steamship Terminal*
Pencil, Watercolor on White Paper, 17 x 24 inches, Senior Design, 1930

James Lister Skinner, *A Christopher Wren Steeple*
Pencil, Watercolor on White Paper, 39.5 x 60 inches, Junior Design, 1934

Julian Hoke Harris (1909-1987) earned a Bachelor of Science in Architecture from Georgia Tech in 1928, and then studied sculpture at the Pennsylvania Academy of the Fine Arts in Philadelphia from 1930 to 1933. He returned to Atlanta to work as a sculptor and to teach in the Architecture Program as a professor from 1936 to 1972. His sculptures may be found on buildings throughout the southeastern United States, as well as on the Georgia Tech campus, including the entry facade of the East Architecture Building.

William Addkison, *Temple of Neptune*, Pencil, Watercolor on White Paper, 35 x 24 inches, Freshman Design, 1934

A FIVE-YEAR PROFESSIONAL DEGREE

Georgia Tech's 1934 course catalog, the *Bulletin*, first described a new, expanded Architecture Program for students intending to become licensed practitioners. The *Bulletin* read: "The new 5-year curriculum in Architecture as contained in this catalogue goes into effect beginning September 1934. Students who intend to enter the Department of Architecture should have two units in French for admission. As heretofore, they will be enrolled in the Department upon entering as Freshmen. At the beginning of the Sophomore year, they will be called upon to select either the Design option or the Structural option. Both of these options lead to the degree of Bachelor of Science at the end of a four-year course. For those who select option No. 1, the Design option, and intend to become practicing architects, a 5th year will be given leading to the degree of the Bachelor of Architecture. For those who may wish to hold a position in almost any branch of the building industry other than that of an architect, either four-year option will give men training to fit them to become useful employees in an architects' organization. Option No. 2 (architectural construction) should prove attractive to men who wish to prepare themselves for the contracting business. The fifth year is for men whose ambition it is to become architects, and only such men who complete the five-year course will receive a degree in Architecture."

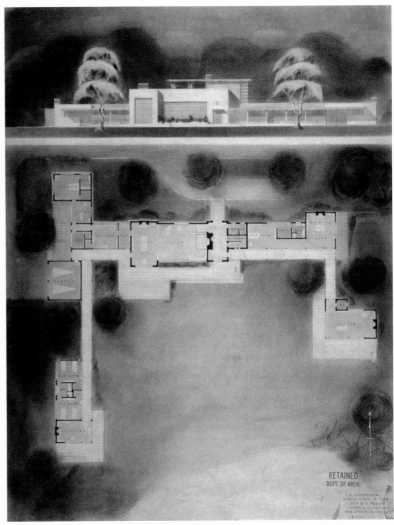

James Alan Stenhouse, *Outdoor Stage*
Watercolor on White Paper, 17.5 x 22.5 inches, Senior Design, 1933

George Raymor Edmondson, *A Summer Residence for a Popular Author*
Pencil, Chalk, Watercolor on White Paper, 28.5 x 36.5 inches, Junior Design, 1934

THE ARCHITECTURE PROGRAM DURING THE GREAT DEPRESSION

The Great Depression of the 1930s was a time of diminished opportunities at Georgia Tech and in society generally. Students, hard-pressed to purchase supplies, conserved paper by drawing on both sides (an example is James Stenhouse's work above). The dwindling employment opportunities for architects reflected a reduced demand for new construction, particularly in the South. But some students found employment under President Roosevelt's New Deal public works programs. Modernism prevailed under federal sponsorship, and while some projects showed traces of the classical proportions, they lacked ornamentation and detail. An example of this shift is illustrated on the Georgia Tech campus between the more traditional Civil Engineering Building (Harold Bush-Brown, 1939) and the Hinman Research Building (Paul M. Heffernan, 1939), which was the first modern building to be constructed on campus.

These years saw heightened pressure on Georgia Tech to abandon its Beaux-Arts traditions. A visit from representatives of the Association of Collegiate Schools of Architecture revealed the changing attitude from study of the classical past towards architecture sympathetic to functional problems of the day. The committee singled out a required sophomore analytique drawing of the classical elements, criticizing its persistence in architectural education and irrelevance in a changing society. Subsequently, the requirement was moved to the freshman year and then eventually was dropped. "In the 1930s at Georgia Tech," Bush-Brown wrote, "I had no idea that the gradual changes we were experiencing would turn into an architectural revolution."

J. A. Hearon, *A Restaurant in the Air*, BAID Second Medal, 1929, Courtesy of Van Alen Institute's Design Competitions Archive

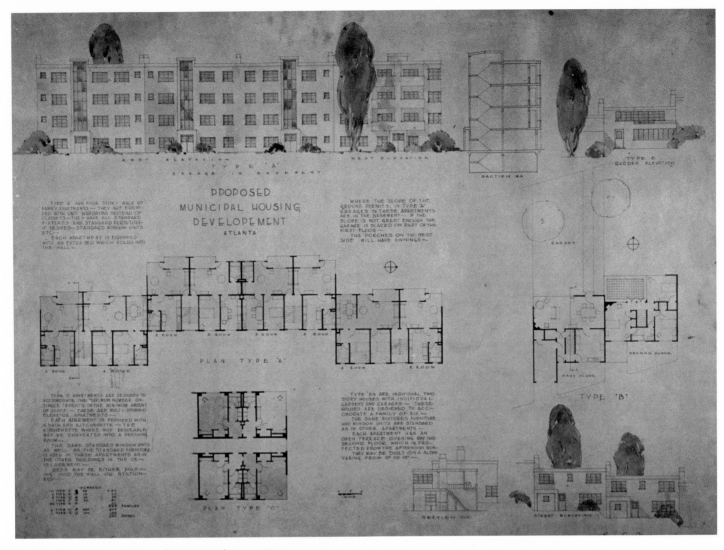

Hugh Stubbins, *A Proposed Municipal Housing Development*, 1933

Francis P. Smith, a former head of the Department of Architecture and a practicing architect at the time, recognized the talent of Hugh Stubbins (1912-2006), a 1933 graduate of the Bachelor of Science in Architecture. While at Georgia Tech, Stubbins was a leader in academics and prevailed in studio work as a recipient of the AIA student medal as well as the Alpha Rho Chi medal. Smith recommended him for a scholarship for graduate studies at Harvard; however, the application required examples of traditional, well-defined styles of the classical origin. Stubbins considered himself a modernist and, along with most of the student body, did not possess a single example of the classical style in the collection of his student work. The students had already responded to the shift in architectural education. Unlike many other disciplines, the architecture student had the ability to set the pace of a stylistic reform. The Bauhaus school of thought was a relatively new model, though some skilled students recognized and achieved this new theory in their designs. However, schools of architecture across the nation continued to offer curriculum based on the organization of programs issued by the Beaux-Arts Institute of Design. In this system, student work was selected by faculty to be sent to New York and judged by notable architectural figures in academia and the profession. The award-winning projects were selected from the ensemble of talented submissions from Eastern, Southern, and Midwestern schools. In 1940, the Department of Architecture received a medal (the University Medal by the Societes des Architectes Diplomas par le Gouvernement Francais, Groupe Americain) for best average rankings on their student work submitted and judged in 1939.

Stubbins earned a graduate degree from Harvard's Graduate School of Design in 1935, later continuing as a Professor of Architecture. He also became the founding principal of Stubbins Associates, Inc. of Cambridge; and in 1967, his firm was among the first to receive an AIA Architectural Firm Award.

LEFT: Cecil Alexander, *China Ink Study*
Freshman Design, 1933

BELOW: James Harrison Finch, *Theater Facade*
Watercolor, Pencil on White Paper, 39.5 x 27 inches
Senior Design, 1936

Richard Robert Caswell, *An Open Air Museum*
Pencil, Watercolor on White Paper
37.5 x 32.5 inches, 1936

James Harrison Finch, *A Design for a Facade*
Pencil, Watercolor on White Paper
40 x 27.5 inches, Senior Design, 1936

James Harrison "Bill" Finch (left) received a Bachelor of Science in Architecture in 1936. He was a recipient of the Alpha Rho Chi Award, which awarded a monetary scholarship to the most outstanding architecture student.

In 1948, he formed a partership with Miller Barnes (Bachelor of Science in Architecture, 1932) in the firm of Finch and Barnes. This later evolved into the prestigious and successful FABRAP firm, formed mostly by Georgia Tech graduates of the Department of Architecture.

Mac Alfred Cason, *A Skating Rink*, Ink on White Paper, 34 x 24 inches, Senior Design, First Prize, 1940

INTRODUCING THE COMBINATION COURSE

The professional degree, which was introduced in 1934, was not the only major curriculum change. By 1940, students could also combine the Bachelor of Science and Bachelor of Architecture degrees into one, five-year professional course of study. The description read: "By taking additional courses during at least one summer session, it is possible to take Option 2 receiving the Bachelor of Science degree with a major in architectural engineering at the expiration of four years and at the same time qualify to receive the Bachelor of Arch degree at the end of the fifth year. A special program of courses should be determined with the approval of the Head of the Department by the end of the Freshman Year" (*Bulletin*, 1940).

But fewer students could take advantage of these changes. While the national economic situation was improving by the late 1930s, enrollments remained low. The number of students who graduated in 1940 was just nineteen, up from just eight in 1937, but still below pre-Depression peaks. The Architecture Department, like Georgia Tech as a whole, would soon face war-related demands for military recruits, keeping enrollment low through mid-1940s. Further, when the war came, the government deemed design "non-essential," so those students who were left could only take the architectural engineering option. These degree requirements focused on study of the history of architecture, "work of construction in practical form," and courses in building materials and construction supplemented by field trips to quarries and brickyards.

Mac Alfred Cason, *A Submarine Base*, Second Place, 33rd Paris Prize
Pencil, Watercolor on White Paper, 33.5 x 24 inches, Fifth Year Design, 1940

WORLD WAR II

In February 1942, federal government authorities in Washington requested that universities change the school calendar from the regular semester system of nine months to an accelerated twelve-month trimester system, to which Georgia Tech consented. In effect, this plan enabled a student to complete a regular four-year course of study in only three years, allowing them to leave for military service sooner. As the architecture curriculum was not listed under engineering courses, architecture students were at a disadvantage in enlisting with the Selective Service System (war training). Some students, however, did enlist for service before completing the requirements for the five-year Bachelor of Architecture degree. However, receiving the five-year rather than the four-year distinction denoted eligibility for the Certificate of Proficiency (for professional practice). The five-year Bachelor of Architecture degree was given in the completion of five consecutive years of study, though students who left for military service during their matriculation were allowed to finish the requirements of this degree upon their return.

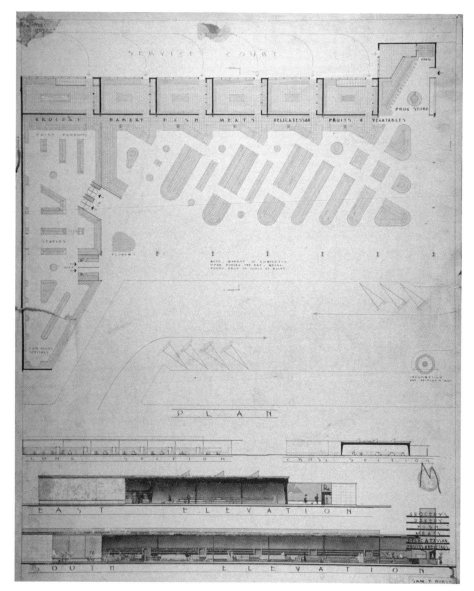

Samuel Thomas Hurst, *A Public Market*
Opaque Color on White Paper, 31 x 40 inches, Senior Design, 1941

William Pope Barney (1890-1970) received his Bachelor of Science in Architecture in 1911, at the age of twenty. His senior thesis was entitled "An American Academy in Rome." During his college years, he served on the *Blueprint* board; he was president of the Institute's Architectural Society and winner of the Atlanta Architectural Arts League prize membership for 1911. He continued his architectural education at the University of Pennsylvania, where he received his second Bachelor of Science in Architecture in 1913. He led a distinguished professional career that included receiving the AIA Gold Medal for Architecture (Davis, Dunlap & Barney of Philadelphia) for his American Bank & Trust Co. building in Philadelphia in 1929. He also served in both the U.S. Army Engineers in World War I and as a lieutenant colonel in the Army Air Corps in World War II. His personal quotation in the 1911 *Blueprint* read: "His only books were woman's look and folly all they taught him."

The Administrations of
Harold Bush-Brown and Paul M. Heffernan

Robert M. Craig

Perhaps no pair of buildings better reflects the transition in architecture and architectural education that took place during the administration of Harold Bush-Brown as the Head of Architecture at Georgia Tech than Brittain Dining Hall (1928) and the Architecture Building (1952). Bush-Brown characterized this transition in the character of the architecture school, as a shift "from Beaux Arts to Bauhaus," and he called it something of a revolution.[1] The development is evident in the different character of student drawings in the first four decades of the school's history, in changes in the curriculum at the school as well as a change of values embodied in these two landmarks of Georgia Tech campus architecture.

At Brittain Hall, Bush-Brown presents the campus with what the Beaux-Arts would call a building of caractère—that is, a structure embodying values beyond mere function, in this case a dining hall serving meals. Flanking the towered entry is an arcade, something of a cloister walk, adorned with sculpted heads which make clear Brittain Hall's didactic purpose. Here, Georgia Tech students are presented with a history of science and the arts, indeed a summary of the very curriculum, institute-wide, at Georgia Tech. Julian Harris, a 1924 graduate of the architecture program, and the same sculptor who created the Pygmalion figure (1953) that now adorns the entry to the Architecture Building, was commissioned in 1933 to carve ten corbel heads along the arcade of Brittain Hall, representing four sciences, three fields of engineering and mathematics, and three fields of arts and crafts. By reference, these carvings provided Georgia Tech students with a who's who in the history of the "best which has been thought and said in the world"—a phrase, by the way, that is Matthew Arnold's definition of culture.[2] They also happened to represent the subjects taught at Georgia Tech.[3]

Inside, the dining room itself is a great hall, a community room in the tradition of manorial great halls, whose secular themes contributed to this same didactic purpose of Bush-Brown's architecture. At the south end of the hall is Julian Harris's student project for a stained-glass window, a cathedral window in the tradition of a secular Cathedral of Learning.[4] The subject is Georgia Tech's curriculum, projected in glass even before it was carved in stone outside. At the bottom of the window are seven figures, from left to right, representing textiles, commerce, architecture, engineering, chemistry, aeronautical engineering, and ceramics. Engineering, of course, is in the center. Above him, the three dominant figures of the window are Mechanical Engineering (a robed ancient figure holding a classical temple, and also featuring a pyramid, a domed edifice, and shrine with dome and minarets above, representing the past), Electrical Engineering (a student robed in academic regalia—is that Tech Tower above?— and representing the present) and Civil Engineering (a worker, the common man, the hands-on man who builds the future, and that features a ship, bridge, factory, and skyscraper above him).[5] It's all here in full-bodied "representational" art, in the sense that traditional, pre-Modernist architecture is grounded in symbol and precedent which brings meaning.

What Bush-Brown would call the slow revolution bubbling up at Georgia Tech and leading to the distinctly different aesthetic of the Architecture Building finds its genesis at this very moment—that is, the early to mid-1930s. By 1952, a new design partner, Paul M. Heffernan, was fully engaged in Bush-Brown's architectural firm, and with respect to Bush-Brown's transition from Beaux-Arts to Bauhaus, the Architecture Building is quintessentially "Bauhaus." To say so would not have pleased its designer, Heffernan, who insisted to this author when we talked about his building, that "functionalist" would be a better stylistic label, and of course, he is correct. But it is hard not to recall the 1925 Bauhaus Building in Dessau in analyzing the functional zoning that informed Heffernan's Architecture Building design, where the workshops and classrooms and the administration and circulation "bridge" are given their respective zones and expressions which are determined by use.

The irony, perhaps, was that Paul M. Heffernan himself had studied at the Ecole des Beaux-Arts in the 1930s, following his winning of the 28th Paris Prize in 1935. However, Heffernan's 1934 Harvard University project for an Airport Station is absolutely current in addressing a contemporary building type and is stylistically current in its streamlined moderne aesthetic. This project by Heffernan dates from merely six years after Brittain Hall, and as a student at Harvard, the young Heffernan was already aware of a changing world in architecture.

CLOCKWISE FROM TOP LEFT: South window, Brittain Dining Hall, student project by Julian Hoke Harris [design, 1924; executed by Lamb Stained Glass Studio, New York, completed by 1932]; Brittain Dining Hall, Bush-Brown and Gailey, 1927-1928; Sculpted head, Michelangelo [The Fine Arts/Architecture], by Julian Hoke Harris, 1934, Brittain Dining Hall, photographs courtesy of Robert M. Craig; Architecture Building, Bush-Brown, Gailey, and Heffernan, 1952

Harold Bush-Brown, in writing about the design transition at Georgia Tech during these years, has noted that "a noticeable change in outlook began to emerge in the way in which many students attacked their design problems" (Bush-Brown, 32). When former Head of Architecture Francis P. Smith returned to serve on a design jury, he recognized the talents of one student in particular, Hugh Stubbins (Class of 1933), and Smith sought to recommend Stubbins for a scholarship for graduate studies at Smith's alma mater, the University of Pennsylvania. Smith "emphasized that the application must include examples of traditional, well-defined styles, preferably classical." As Bush-Brown recounts, "not a single example of classical or any historical style by [Stubbins] could be found. . .not even the required analytique . . . In other words . . . the young man in question, even in the early 1930s, was a modernist, an avant garde."[6]

Most of the student projects at Georgia Tech, however, were still traditional, given the studio drawing assignments and programs. However, some exceptional modern work was already emerging by the 1930s from classmates of Hugh Stubbins and those who immediately followed. Here is some conservative modern student work from the decade, which, looking back, appears current for the mid-Depression years with their modernized classical forms. However, seniors from the class of 1936, James H. "Bill" Finch and Willard Lamberson, display a distinctly modern, volumetric image for their successful entries in the Illuminating Engineering Society Prize project for "An Automobile Salon." Lamberson won a first medal scholarship for his Cadillac showroom, while Finch took top honors winning the first prize for his Bentley showroom. Both projects were published in *The Bulletin of the Beaux-Arts Institute of Design* (BAID).[7] A few years after these student projects, when Atlanta hosted the national BAID competitions, Bush-Brown has recorded, "without exception all the drawings sent in by various schools were modern in design."[8]

Ralph Slay's entry in 1936 for the BAID Class A Project I for "A Summer Hotel," which won a Second Medal, reflects the two forces at play in the Georgia Tech studios in shaping projects during the period. In plan, Slay organizes the approach, vestibule, lobby, and lounge of his hotel in Beaux-Arts enfilade, establishing significant cross axes at the lobby center. But Slay dresses the whole as a nautical Moderne asymmetrical and functionalist composition with portholes, terraces much like promenade decks, ship rails, and the generally ornament-less, volumetric, and orderly structured forms of the International Style. Such Early Modern design, the "new architecture" of the Europeans, had been introduced to Americans at the Museum of Modern Art four years earlier.

It is not necessary to be reminded that Walter Gropius arrived at Harvard in 1937, that the same year Maholy Nagy arrived in Chicago to head up a New Bauhaus and that Mies Van der Rohe became Director of the Armour Institute (later the Illinois Institute of Technology) in 1938. At this same historic moment, in the fall of 1938, Paul Heffernan arrived at Georgia Tech.

Heffernan's first campus building was the new Research Experiment Station Building, built in 1939 and later named Hinman. Soon after the completion of Hinman, World War II broke out, and the student population in architecture was reduced to barely a handful. When the war ended, and students like my good friend Joseph Smith returned to complete their degrees, there were more than 400 architecture students and a desperate need for new faculty. Bush-Brown hired three young design teachers from the Harvard Graduate School of Design, by then headed by Gropius: D. J. "Jim" Edwards, Thomas Godfrey, and Samuel T. Hurst. The latter would work with Heffernan in designing the Wesley Foundation Building on campus in 1960. Georgia Tech's late 1940s new faculty were described as "mini-Gropius-ites," and the revolution from Beaux-Arts to Bauhaus was complete. Heffernan sealed it by building the Textile Engineering Building in 1948.

Harold Bush-Brown has remarked about the new faculty's "enthusiasm for the new approach to the teaching of architecture,"[9] and he suggested they were effective in attracting modern leaders as guest lecturers and visiting design critics to Georgia Tech. And what a notable group of early modernists these post-war visitors to Georgia Tech were: Walter Gropius, Marcel Breuer, I.M. Pei, and in the spring of 1952, Frank Lloyd Wright.

The Architecture Building embodies very different values than those of such earlier campus structures as Brittain Hall. First, as Heffernan described it, the Architecture Building is a functionalist building, with public spaces and intellectual zones as well as a creative studio wing where the design work takes place. However, like Harris's corbels and stained glass at Brittain Hall, the Architecture Building also bears witness to emerging changes in the School's curriculum, new programs of study that generated the need for a new building in the first place.

With respect to functional zoning, Heffernan's 1952 Architecture Building presents its public face in its south block where a 300-seat auditorium provided a venue for the larger community and public. As an historian, I find Heffernan's original design for this space, with its undulating sidewalls, offers an interesting comparison to his 1935 Paris Prize winning entry for an auditorium in an opera house. Above our auditorium in the Architecture Building, a large exhibition gallery offered space for traveling exhibits and for display of student work. The Director's office was prominently sited, immediately off the main entry stair and with its own papal balcony from where the head of school could pontificate to gathering communicants, those student pilgrims gathered before the shrine of architecture.

A connecting bridge provided additional jury space along a corridor, the Jean Cohen Gallery now, and pinups have historically been "on the bridge." The bridge also housed the Architecture Library, the campus's only satellite subject library. Finally, the north wing was for classrooms, faculty offices, and studios. The south front of the studio wing overlooked the courtyard and was marked by brise soleils as screens against the direct glare of the sun, and the north elevation, with its wonderful four levels of stacked ribbon windows, brought a desirable even north light into the studio spaces. On the ground floor was industrial design, with its workshop containing tools and equipment for making models, templates, and products emerging from student projects in a new field of study, industrial design, as well as in architecture. A hierarchy of architecture studios was above, culminating on the top floor where senior or fifth-year architectural design work took place. Here Heffernan provided a mezzanine level as an overlook for students, much like galleries for medical students in an operating theater, so that the rest of the School could observe the "surgical operations" below, that is, the critiques of the best work in the senior studio. Everything about the building's planning gives evidence of this functional zoning, a plan that addresses, first and foremost, the needs of the school's changing curricula.

A final argument can be made that Heffernan's Architecture Building is also an embodiment of the programs of study, educational curriculum development, and professional disciplines underway at the turn of the 1950s. A new Architecture Building was needed at Georgia Tech not only because of the dramatic increase in the number of students studying architecture and its related fields after World War II, but also because of changes in the School's programs of study, and, in fact, funds that helped pay for the building were solicited in support of curriculum development not capital improvement.

To demonstrate the final point regarding the changing curriculum and how these student projects and Heffernan's campus buildings—both Textile Engineering and Architecture—reflect a real turning point, one should consider these parallel dates in curriculum development here. When Harold Bush-Brown first came to Georgia Tech in 1922, the school offered a Two-Year Certificate in Architecture and one bachelor's degree, a Bachelor of Science in Architecture. About the time Hugh Stubbins left Georgia Tech for Harvard to join Heffernan as a student there (a dozen years later), Georgia Tech moved to a five-year program, awarding its first Bachelor of Architecture degree to Arthur Neal Robinson, Jr. In 1939, the year of Heffernan's first campus building, the Hinman Research Building, the School granted a Bachelor of Science in Architectural Engineering and would do so until about 1947. In fact, in 1941 Bush-Brown listed himself as Head of the School of Architectural Engineering, and in 1942, some Bachelor of Science degrees at graduation distinguished between architectural design and architectural engineering. The following year, the 1943 school yearbook, the *Blueprint*, started listing students in industrial design. After World War II, the number of students studying at the architecture school jumped to more than 400, and the three Gropius-ites were hired to join the faculty. Heffernan taught senior design. And then in 1952, the Architecture Building was designed to house an entirely new approach to architecture and its related disciplines.

That same year Hin Bredendieck was hired to teach industrial design; his diploma was from the Bauhaus. The next year, 1953, the first Master of Architecture degree was awarded: it went to Doc Gailey's son who had previously earned a Bachelor of Science in Architectural Engineering at Georgia Tech in 1943 and a Bachelor of Science in Architecture in 1951.[10] The next year, the first Master of City Planning degree was awarded. Two years later, in 1956, the elder Doc Gailey retired—he had taught at the architecture school since 1912 when Francis Smith hired him, and then in 1956, Harold Bush-Brown also retired. A new Director of the School of Architecture was immediately named: it was Paul M. Heffernan. Three years later, in 1959, the first Bachelor of Science in Industrial Design was granted, and in the same year, a Bachelor of Science in Building Construction.

Heffernan said his building was functionalist. On both counts, it was. It was a direct embodiment of the program, zoned in discrete sections of the building to address particular needs. And it served dramatically expanding new programs at the architecture school, which was just beginning to offer these broader studies in architecture, city planning, industrial design, and building construction.

—Robert M. Craig, PhD, is a Professor of Architecture at Georgia Tech.

NOTES

1. Harold Bush-Brown, *Beaux Arts to Bauhaus and Beyond: An Architect's Perspective.* New York: Watson Guptill Publications, 1976.

2. Matthew Arnold, *Culture and Anarchy*, 1869.

3. The fields of study and historic figures representing each are as follows: Fine Arts—Michelangelo; Textile—Eli Whitney; Ceramics—Luca della Robia; Civil, Mechanical, and Aeronautical Engineering—Leonardo da Vinci; Electrical Engineering—Thomas Edison; Mathematics and Astronomy—Isaac Newton; Chemistry—Antoine-Laurent Lavoisier; Geology—Charles Darwin; Biological Sciences—Aristotle; and Physics—Archimedes.

4. The same year Brittain Hall was built (1928), architect Charles Z. Klauder began his skyscraper known as the Cathedral of Learning for the University of Pittsburgh.

5. Flanking this triad of central figures are two additional pairs: at left, a scribe representing literature (and drama symbolized by the masks of tragedy and comedy) and a medieval knight representing the military; on the right, a Viking sailor representing the Navy and a discus thrower representing athletics.

6. Ibid., 34. Joseph Esherick has described a similar phenomenon at Berkeley, as students discovered Le Corbusier and European modernism even before the faculty seemed to, and where the design school ultimate caught up. Joseph Esherick, "Architectural Education in the Thirties and Seventies: A Personal View" in Spiro Kostov, ed., *The Architect: Chapters in the History of the Profession*, New York: Oxford University Press, 1977.

7. *The Bulletin of the Beaux-Arts Institute of Design*, XII: 6 (April, 1936), 15 and 18.

8. Bush-Brown, 34, 36.

9. Ibid., 43.

10. James Herbert "Doc" Gailey, (Master of Science in Architecture, University of Pennsylvania) began his forty-four-year career at Georgia Tech in 1912 as an instructor in the new architecture school then headed by Francis Smith. His son Charles Malcolm Gailey first served as an instructor at Georgia Tech during the academic year 1955-6, just as his father retired.

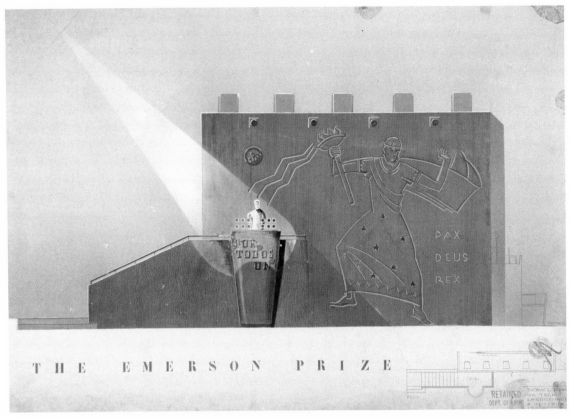

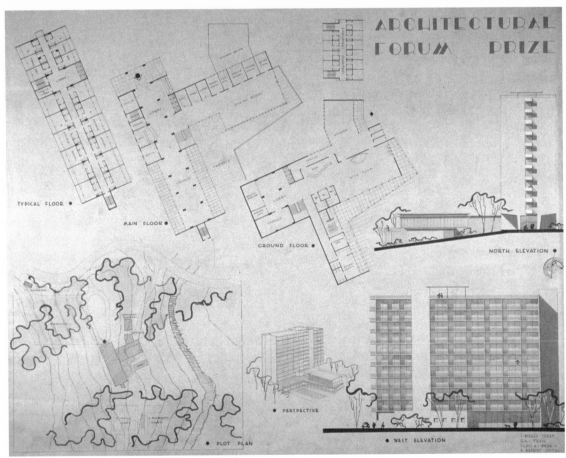

TOP: Thomas Edwin Garner, *A Rostrum for a Pan American Congress*
First Place, Emerson Prize, Watercolor on White Paper, 40 x 28.5 inches, Senior Design, 1942

BOTTOM: Charles Birney Curry, *A Resort Hotel*
Pencil, Watercolor on White Paper, 39.5 x 31 inches, Freshman Design, 1942

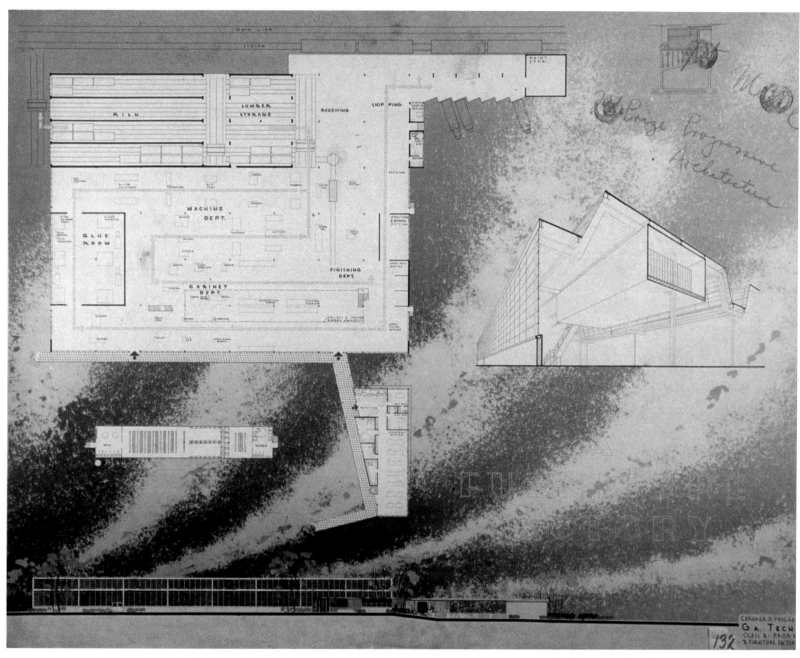

Caraker Denham Paschal, *A Furniture Factory*, Second Prize, *Progressive Architecture*
Ink, Watercolor on White Paper, 39.5 x 31 inches, Senior Design, 1943

Prior to World War II, the enrollment in the Department of Architecture averaged 125 students per year. Because of voluntary enlistment and the draft during the war years, student enrollment dropped to a low of twenty-two students and four faculty: Professor Harold Bush-Brown, Professor James H. Gailey, Associate Professor Paul M. Heffernan, and Instructor Ed Moulthrop. Like the rest of the nation, students, faculty, and alumni contributed to the war effort. Architecture faculty taught courses in other subjects; for example, Professor Bush-Brown attended a two-week camouflage program at Fort Belvoir, Virginia, and conveyed his knowledge of camouflage design to Georgia Tech students. Architects found their skills of use for war service in the Civil Engineer Corps, the Seabees, and the Navy. Among the armed forces, however, only the Navy considered architecture to be one of the vital curricula worth subsidizing. This lack of federal support along with the drop in enrollment led the Georgia Tech administration to temporarily postpone the program in architecture and in its place approved a five-year degree in architectural engineering. This new architectural engineering degree was awarded to ten architecture students after completing only nine semesters of coursework. After the war, Tech eliminated the architectural engineering degree and restored the pre-war architecture curriculum.

Georgia Tech Army First Battalion, 1942

Camouflage Program, 1942

With the end of World War II, overall student enrollment increased dramatically causing reconsideration of the basic organization of the Institute. In 1945, all degree options in the Architecture Program led to a Bachelor of Science degree (without designation) at the end of four years. For the candidates pursuing an architectural degree, an additional year was required to obtain the Bachelor of Architecture degree designation. The five-year professional degree was not unique to Georgia Tech at the time, as it was already offered in the curriculum of several architecture schools across the country. In 1946, the divisions of the academic school year switched from the three-quarter system implemented during World War II back to the two-semester system that was in place before the war. In 1948, under the leadership of President Blake R. Van Leer, Georgia Tech underwent a reorganization that included a restructuring of its colleges and a new name—the Georgia Institute of Technology. These changes resulted in the creation of the School of Architecture, which also offered courses in industrial design and the light construction industry. This administrative designation made it comparable to other professional schools within the College of Engineering.

OPPOSITE, TOP: Joseph Warner Morgan, *A Shore Restaurant*, Pencil, Watercolor on White Paper, 40 x 31 inches, Senior Design, 1944

OPPOSITE, BOTTOM: Johnnie Serafino Fornara, *A Weekend House*, Watercolor on White Paper, 40 x 31.5 inches, Senior Design, 1943

PERSPECTIVE

INTERIOR

SECTION

ELEVATION

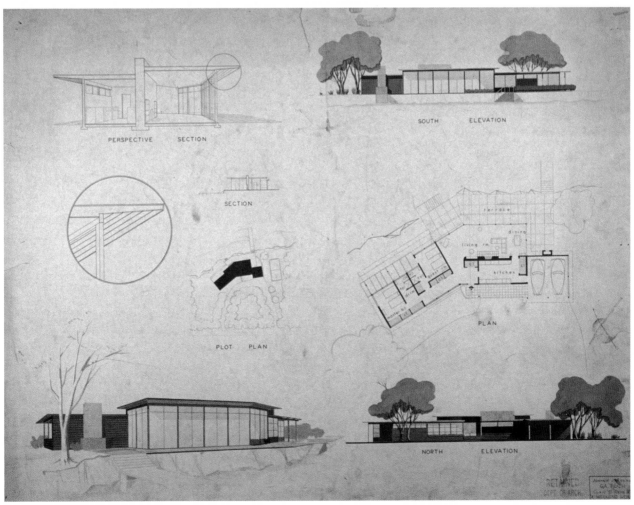

PERSPECTIVE SECTION

SOUTH ELEVATION

SECTION

PLOT PLAN

PLAN

NORTH ELEVATION

In June of 1942, head of architecture Harold Bush-Brown mentioned several planning matters in a report to President Marion L. Brittain for the Board of Regents stating that "the government, it appears, is looking forward to conditions of the post-war situation…This means establishment and adoption of a master plan for future development [at Georgia Tech] as an initial and major step," as quoted in *Engineering the New South* (1985). Bush-Brown established a hierarchy of project plans based on the needs of the campus. The most immediate priorities involved planning for equipment upgrades, more land, and new buildings to house the architecture, chemistry, physics, and textile engineering programs. Other projects in the framework of the developing master plan allowed for a new mechanical engineering building, a main campus library, hospital facilities, and additional dormitories. The long-term planning elements incorporated the projected needs in buildings, space, and services in future growth of the campus. The Board of Regents authorized President Brittain to engage the architecture department at Georgia Tech, under Bush-Brown's direction, to draw up a long-range development plan, with the cost of preparing the plan coming from profits earned by radio station WGST. With these funds, Bush-Brown established an Office of Long-Range Development within the Department of Architecture in 1943.

MASTER PLAN AT GEORGIA TECH

In 1944, the firm of Bush-Brown and Gailey, Architects, with associate architects R. L. Aeck and P. M. Heffernan, created a master campus plan (shown on right) to accommodate the projected increase in students who would enroll once World War II ended. As the campus renovations were under way, the School of Architecture moved into temporary buildings constructed to accommodate the large number of students in the program and faculty that were employed to design for the campus expansion. The master plan projected growth in a northerly direction and indicated that the teaching and working areas would remain in the west [now considered central] campus, with living areas to the east, and recreation and athletic areas located in between. Three of the proposed buildings that were given priority were: a main library, a building for the School of Architecture, and a new Textile Engineering building. All three would be built in the next decade following the modernist designs of faculty member and future Director of Architecture P. M. Heffernan.

R.L. Aeck, BS ARCH 1936, an associate architect in the firm of Bush-Brown and Gailey, Architects, R. L. Aeck and P. M. Heffernan, Associate Architects, constructed drawings and a model for the central educational area of the Georgia Tech campus expansion to evaluate whether they would be served by roadways, walks, or parking lots. Also, the June 1948 issue of *Progressive Architecture* published the designs for the modern addition to the stadium, created by the firm of Bush-Brown and Gailey, with associate architects P. M. Heffernan and R. L. Aeck. Aeck was the main designer responsible for the modern addition of the West Stands at Grant Field.

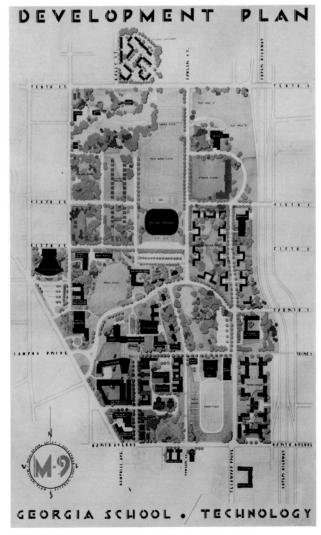

Faculty with campus planning models, 1943

Harold Bush-Brown

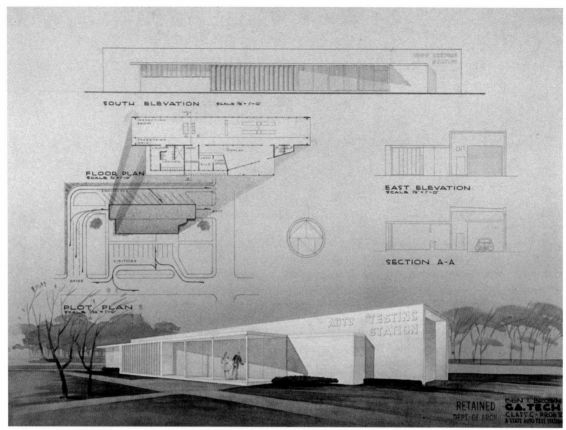

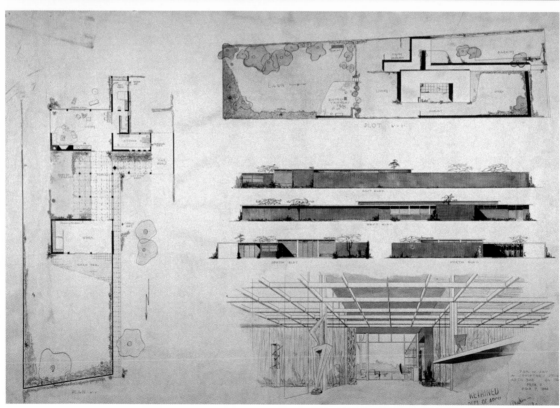

TOP: Benjamin I. Brown, *A State Auto Testing Station*
Color Ink, Watercolor, Air Brush on Paper, 30 x 22 inches
Junior Design, 1947

BOTTOM: Thom W. Jay, *A Sculptor's Studio*
Ink, Watercolor on White Paper; 37.5 x 26 inches
1948

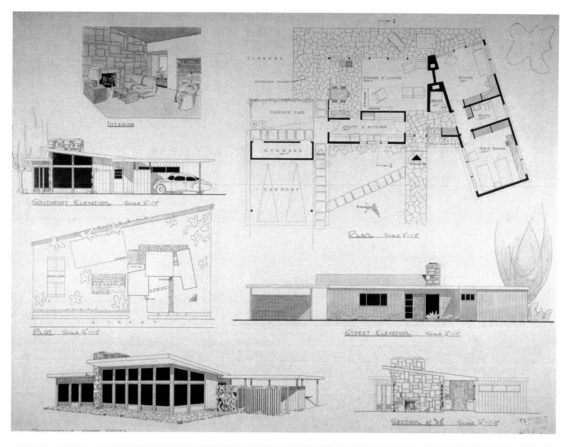

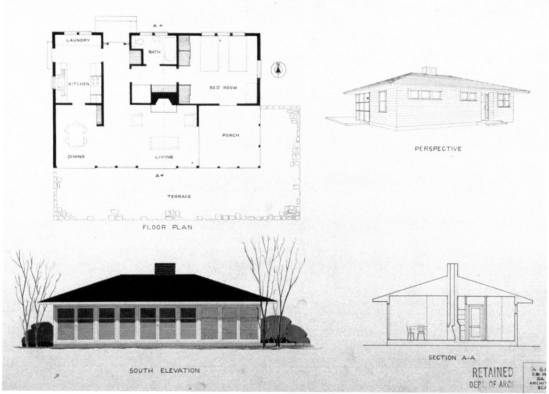

TOP: Leslie E. Trotter, *A Small House*
Ink, Watercolor on Paper, 39.5 x 31 inches
Sophomore Design, 1948

BOTTOM: C. B. Winslette, *A GI House*, First Mention
Sepia Ink, Watercolor on Paper, 30 x 20 inches
Senior Design, 1947

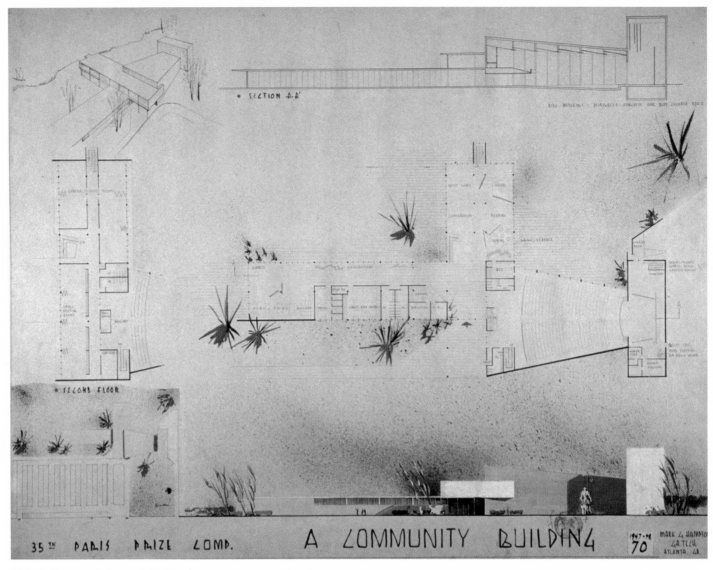

Mark G. Hampton, *A Community Building*
Pencil, Watercolor on White Paper, 40 x 31 inches
35th Paris Prize Competition, Junior Design, 1948

AFTER THE WAR

Notes from the *Bulletin* (1948-1949)

There exists a shortage of men in the profession of architecture and a need of trained personnel in the whole field of building industry. The School of Architecture is, however, handicapped by lack of space and more men are enrolling than can be carried along to completion of the course. This is especially true of those indicating preference for the first two options. Every effort is being made to provide an education for men who have the special qualifications regarded as desirable and prerequisite to success. Those who are sure of their choice will be given every encouragement, but those in doubt or those whose scholastic record indicates a low average, are advised to seek other fields and thereby avoid disappointment and waste of time. All students entering the Department should take interest and aptitude tests, and those wishing to pursue the course of instruction under Options 1 and 2, these tests will be a prerequisite of enrollment the beginning of the Junior Year. Any student failing to qualify for Option 1 and 2 may continue in Option 4.

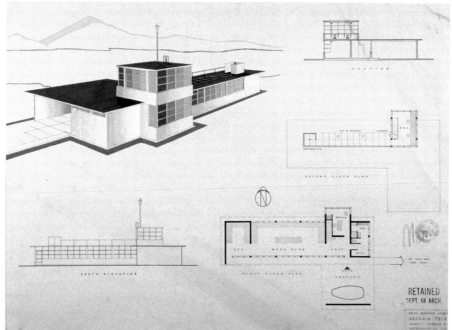

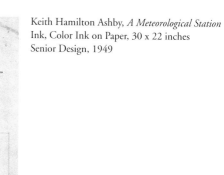

Keith Hamilton Ashby, *A Meteorological Station*
Ink, Color Ink on Paper, 30 x 22 inches
Senior Design, 1949

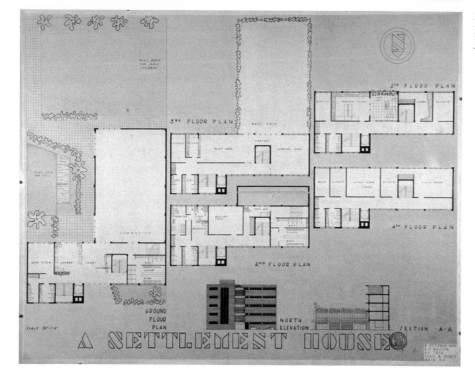

Ernest O. Mastin, *A Settlement House*
Ink, Airbrush on White Paper, 39.5 x 31 inches
Junior Design, 1949

According to Harold Bush-Brown, Frank Lloyd Wright was the only architect capable of filling the auditorium. Following his lecture in 1952, Wright graciously made himself available for meeting the students of the School of Architecture. John C. Portman, B ARCH 1950, recalled upon meeting the renowned architect, he asked "What advice do you have for architects today?," and Wright simply answered, "Read [Ralph Waldo] Emerson."

LEFT: Frank Lloyd Wright pictured at an Architectural Society barbecue in 1952

EXPANSION OF THE CURRICULUM

The General Education Board of the Ford Foundation in New York named Georgia Tech's School of Architecture as recipient of funds for an expansion program in 1952. The goal of achieving a national and international reputation in professional design education included expanding the scope and professional orientation of architecture. The State of Georgia matched these funds, at which time the architecture administration recommended the initiation of a graduate course in architecture, degrees in city planning and industrial design, research funds, expansion of the architecture library, and exhibition space. Courses in industrial design and the light construction industry were offered in 1940, leading to the Bachelor of Science degree without designation. Programs for industrial design and building construction were reactivated and given full degree designation in 1952 and 1958, respectively. The first Master of Architecture degree was awarded to Charles Gailey in June 1953, and the master's degree extended the focus to include city planning in 1956 (under the leadership of Howard Menhinick). In 1958, the Bachelor of Architecture degree became the one and only qualifying degree in architecture.

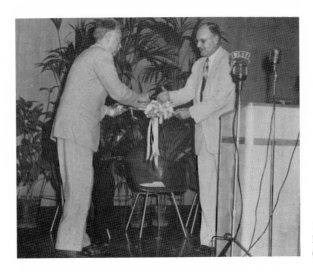

1952 Architecture Building dedication,
Harold Bush-Brown (left) pictured
(published in *Progressive Architecture*, July 1955)

ARCHITECTURE BUILDING

The Georgia Tech administration battled with the issue of whether new campus construction should conform to the traditional style of existing campus buildings or be of the current modern design. Completed in July 1952, the School of Architecture building, designed by P. M. Heffernan, who was now a partner in the firm of Bush-Brown, Gailey, and Heffernan, reflected the combined interests of the partnership—legible Beaux-Arts planning combined with Bauhaus massing and vocabulary. For the first time since the establishment of the program in 1908, the School of Architecture achieved a separate identity from the other engineering disciplines with its significant new building.

In conformance with the master plan, the building design provided sufficient exterior space to avoid a sense of crowding and to allow for future expansion. The initial concept was described in the *Technique* in October 1950, "The building will be of concrete frame construction with a brick veneer. It is of a U-shaped design consisting of a north wing and a south wing with a connecting wing, a concourse between the two main wings. The north wing will have two stories. The building will contain approximately 67,000 square feet, and will be partially air-conditioned. Included in the building will be one lecture hall, one laboratory, four drafting rooms, an exhibition room, a seminar room, nine offices for instructors, two classrooms, offices for the department head, and a library. The library will be located in the connecting wing between the two main wings. The exhibition room will be used to display the designs made by the Architectural students."

CLOCKWISE FROM TOP LEFT: Architecture Library, 1952; Rooftop Terrace, 1952; South Facade, Architecture Building, 1952

Price Gilbert Memorial Library, 1953

CAMPUS ARCHITECTURE

While in the firm of Bush-Brown, Gailey, and Heffernan, P. M. Heffernan aided in the final designs for several campus buildings underway in the Georgia Tech Campus master plan and expansion, including the Architecture Building, the Hinman Research Building, the Smith, Glenn and Tower Dormitories, the Old West Stands of Grant Field, the Bradley Building, the School of Textile Engineering, the Price Gilbert Library, and the State Highway Laboratory. His designs for the familiar and recognizable campus buildings were published in *Progressive Architecture, Architectural Forum, Architectural Record, L'Architecture Francaise*, and *Vitrum*. Since the initiation of the campus master plan, the faculty-led firm of Bush-Brown, Gailey, and Heffernan received favorable publicity at the local level and from national architecture journals for their campus buildings. These buildings became attractions for Georgia Tech visitors and helped faculty and administration to attract students and enhance graduate education and research at Tech. However, in 1953, under threat of a lawsuit, the University System Building Authority and Board of Regents began placing campus projects out for bid after receiving pressure from other architects in the state who thought the faculty was given an unfair advantage in the selection process. Thus, members of the architecture faculty were no longer able to design campus buildings. Alumni could, however, continue to place bids.

Hinman Research Building, 1939

Textile Engineering Building
1951 (razed 2007)

Palazzo Rucellai
Florence
1957

Ospedale
egli Innocenti
Firenze
1957

Travel sketches by Jerry Cooper made during his Fulbright Fellowship, 1956

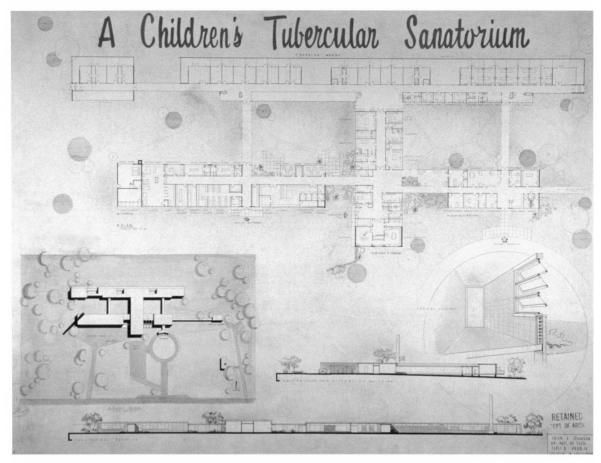

TOP: John Elwyn Johnson, *Children's T.B. Sanatorium*
Ink, Watercolor on White Paper, 39.5 x 30 inches
Senior Design, 1951

BOTTOM: H. E. Dodd, *An Entrance to a Museum*
Pencil, Ink, Watercolor on White Paper, 38.5 x 25 inches
Senior Design, 1954

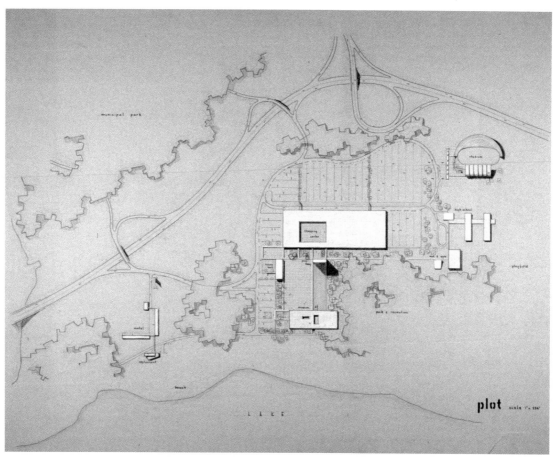

TOP: Roman Antonia Davila, *Museum*
Prisma Color on Light Blue Board, 40 x 30.5 inches
Senior Design, 1956

BOTTOM: Bernard Weinstein, *A Spring House*
Pencil, Ink & Wash on Board, 40 x 30 inches
Sophomore Design, 1956

In 1956, with the retirement of Harold Bush-Brown (1888-1983), Paul M. Heffernan was named director of the School. Heffernan received a bachelor's degree in the Architectural Engineering Program at Iowa State University in 1929, and a Master of Science in Architectural Engineering in 1931. After teaching at Iowa State until 1933, he entered Harvard University to complete his Master of Architecture degree in 1935. He received first prize in the 28th Paris Prize and became an élève (premiére classe), at the Ecole Nationale Superieure des Beaux-Arts, Paris, France, between 1935 and 1938. P. M. Heffernan began teaching at Georgia Tech as an Associate Professor of Architecture in 1938.

BELOW RIGHT, TOP: P. M. Heffernan shown on third floor studio mezzanine in East Architecture Building

BELOW RIGHT, BOTTOM: Photo of Entire School of Architecture faculty, 1956. Professor Paul M. Heffernan (Director), third from left, bottom row; Harold Bush-Brown (former Department Head), third from right, bottom row. Also included in the picture but in no order are: Howard K. Menhinick (Regents' Professor of City Planning), Professor J. H. Gailey (Professor Emeritus); Associate Professors Hin Bredendieck (Industrial Design), Demetrios Polychrone (Structural Design), Richard Pretz, H. Griffith Edwards (Part-time), Julian Harris (Part-time), S. T. Hurst, Isaac Saporta, and Richard Wilson; Assistant Professors Rufus R. Greene, Malcolm G. Little, Robert F. Rabun, Vernon M. Shipley, and George W. Ramey (Part-time); Instructor Norman L. Worrell

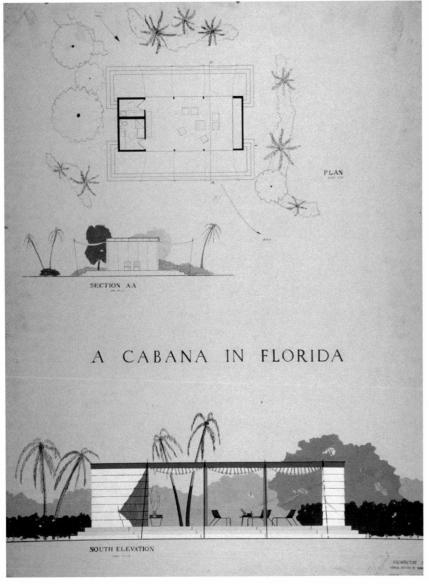

LEFT: William F. Oliver, *A Cabana in Florida*
Ink, Black & White Color on Board, 30 x 40 inches
Freshman Design, 1955

62

Robert Brooks Powell, *A Zoological Park*
Watercolor on Board, 40 x 30 inches
Junior Design, 1955

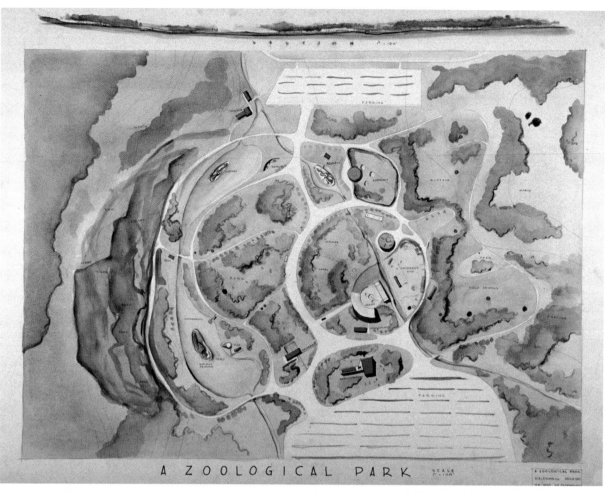

Milt Sweigert
A Municipal Recreation Pier and Marina
Ink, Watercolor on Board, 40 x 30 inches
Senior Design, 1956

On May 28, 1956, the School of Architecture opened an exhibition titled "A Half Century of Architectural Education" that featured work of former Georgia Tech architecture students of the period from 1908 to 1956. Four judges evaluated the over five hundred exhibition entries of alumni professional work and selected sixty pieces. The judges were a distinguished group that included: Paul Heffernan, director-designate of the School of Architecture, Francis P. Smith, former director of the Department of Architecture, Roy C. Jones, former director of Minnesota's Architecture School, and Joseph Hudnut, former dean of Harvard's Graduate School of Design. The School's exhibition director, Associate Professor D.J. Edwards, organized this presentation of professional work as a tribute to former directors of the Architecture Program, including retiring director Harold Bush-Brown and former directors Francis P. Smith (1909-1922) and John L. Skinner (1922-1925). In the accompanying 1956 exhibit catalog, the author Joseph Hudnut observed, "The usages of their profession encourage among architects a perennial optimism. Men who plan cannot be pessimists; and men who build must be confident of the future. Habitually mindful of progressions and constructive imaginings, architects live in a world that is forever transcending—or about to transcend—its mean appearances. Architects play constantly a part in the realization of that world."

ABOVE LEFT: George Heery, BS ARCH 1951, pictured next to his firm's (Heery and Heery) exhibit entry: "Medical Center, Athens, Georgia C. Wilmer Heery '26 and George T. Heery '51 architects"

ABOVE RIGHT: Tom Ventulett received a Bachelor of Science in Architecture in 1957 and a Bachelor of Architecture in 1958, followed by a Master of Architecture from the University of Pennsylvania. In 1968, he co-founded and became the director of design of Thompson, Ventulett, Stainback & Associates, which is internationally recognized and one of the nation's largest architectural firms. Today the College of Architecture's prestigious Thomas W. Ventulett, III Chair in Architectural Design recognizes Ventulett's outstanding professional accomplishments and his commitment to Georgia Tech.

OPPOSITE, TOP: Thomas W. Ventulett, III, *A Community Club for Lake Berkeley*, Pencil, Watercolor on White Paper, 32 x 20 inches, Junior Design, 1957
OPPOSITE, BOTTOM: Ben Cunningham, *Entrance Hall to an Aquarium*, Ink, Watercolor on Board, 40 x 30 inches, Senior Design, 1957

A COMMUNITY CLUB
for LAKE BERKELEY

PERSPECTIVES
ARCH · 303   T.W. VENTULETT

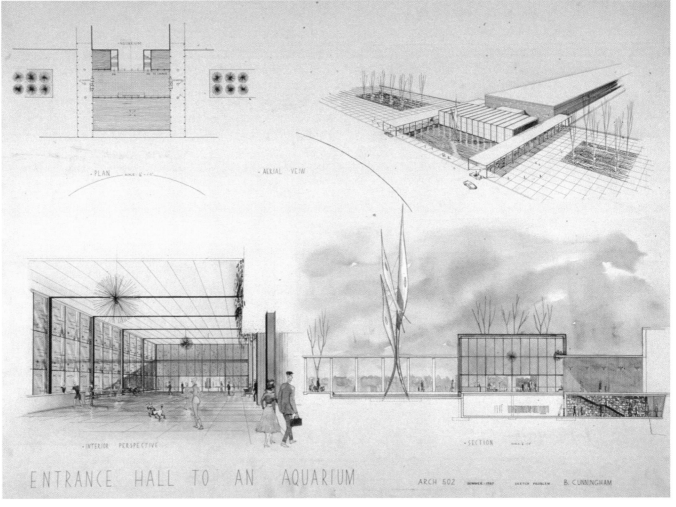

· PLAN ·   · AERIAL VEIW ·

· INTERIOR · PERSPECTIVE ·   · SECTION ·

ENTRANCE HALL TO AN AQUARIUM   ARCH 502   SUMMER·1957   SKETCH PROBLEM   B. CUNNINGHAM

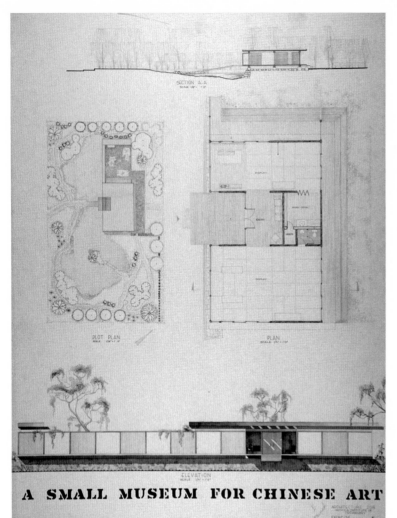

A SMALL MUSEUM FOR CHINESE ART

LEFT: Jimmy Piephoff Chapman, *A Small Museum for Chinese Art*
Ink, Pencil, Watercolor on Board, 30 x 40 inches
Freshman Design, 1958

BELOW: William Jerome Tenison, Jr., *A Fraternity House*
Ink, Watercolor on White Paper, 40 x 29 inches
Sophomore Design, 1959

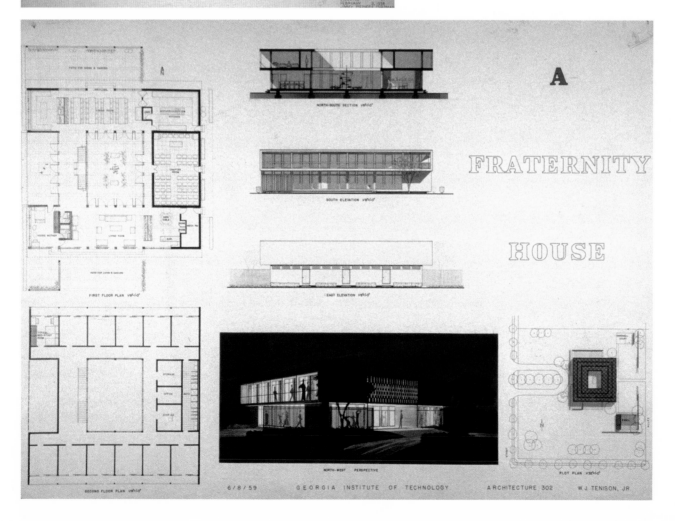

LEFT: William Oliver, *An Aviary*
Pencil, Watercolor on White Paper, 40 x 30 inches
Fifth Year Design, 1960

BELOW: William Kambmeies, *An Oceanarium*
Ink, Watercolor, 29.5 x 20 inches
Fifth Year Design, 1960

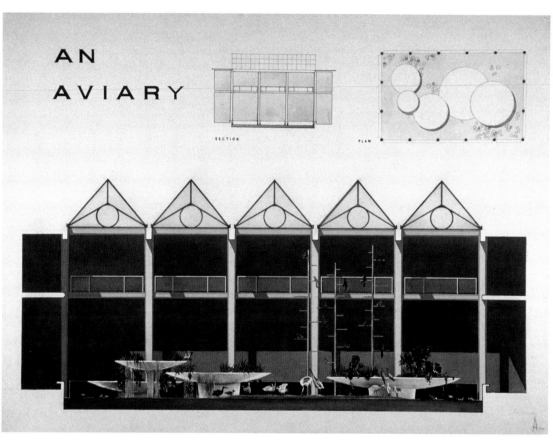

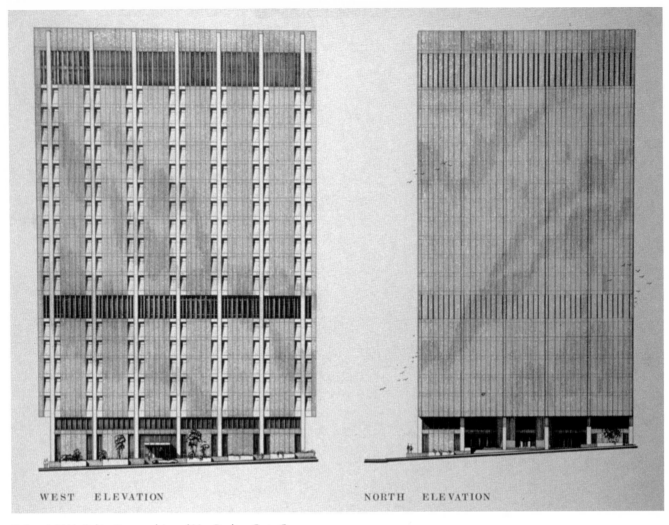

Barbara A. Field, *Fashion Center and Apparel Mart Peachtree Center C*
Ink, Airbrush, Watercolor on Board, 30 x 40 inches, c.1966

WEST ELEVATION   NORTH ELEVATION

WOMEN IN ARCHITECTURE

In 1953, for the first time, Georgia Tech allowed women to matriculate to work toward a degree. Six years later Thera H. Richter became the first woman to earn a degree from the School of Architecture and from Georgia Tech; however, her degree was a Master of City Planning. In the early 1960s, women were admitted to the previously all-male Architecture Program. In 1966, the first women to receive the five-year Bachelor of Architecture degree were Esther Behar and Barbara Field (pictured on right). In 1962, among the approximately 6,000 students enrolled at Georgia Tech, fifty-one were women. By 1966, the number of women had grown to 108, with the total student population of 7,349. Within the next decade, only ten women graduated with a Bachelor of Architecture degree. The overall student population at Georgia Tech during the fall of 2008 was 19,404, with women comprising only 28 percent of students. Of the almost 600 students pursuing a degree in architecture, women make up half of the students.

Barbara Field, B ARCH 1966, said, "I wouldn't have stayed in architecture if everybody hadn't told me I couldn't do it."

Talbot Rex Hamilton, *A Church Community Center*
Ink, Watercolor on White Paper, 40 x 30 inches, Fifth Year Design, 1963

Notes from the *Bulletin*, 1960-1961

The original objective and first aim of the School is to prepare students for the profession of Architecture. The scope of the field is of such breadth in current practice that need is felt not only for men who are strong in design but for others whose interests will be closely integrated with design in structural and mechanical techniques. The training in Architecture is uniform for the first four years with two areas of specialization, Architectural Design and Structural Design, strongly emphasized in the final year. The central core of the curriculum in Architecture is the study of design, with related exercises in drawing, graphics, visual composition, and model building.

Closely allied to design and, insofar as possible, integrated with it are the courses in construction which, in turn, are dependent on the basic requirements of mathematics, physics, and mechanics. Courses in the history and theory of architecture supply a fuller understanding of our architectural heritage, its meaning and impact on contemporary problems. Work of technical importance is offered in building materials, mechanical plant (plumbing, heating, air-conditioning and electrical installations), office and field practice.

The National Architectural Accrediting Board has officially accredited the 5-year course leading to the degree Bachelor of Architecture at the Georgia Institute of Technology.

LEFT: Georgia Tech students gathered in the gym for a meeting with Georgia Tech President Edwin D. Harrison before campus desegregation: "I told them if they couldn't behave, they couldn't stay in school," Harrison recalls (Eugene Griessman et al., *Images and Memories: Georgia Tech, 1885-1985*, 1985).

DESEGREGATION AND SOCIAL CHANGE

In 1957, Edwin D. Harrison replaced Blake Van Leer as Georgia Tech's president. Van Leer had overseen the dramatic growth of the Institute since 1944. During the tenure of these two presidents, numerous social changes occurred without many of the disruptions experienced on other college campuses throughout the South. The Supreme Court ruling in *Brown v. Board of Education* (1954) opened the doors of white schools to students of color. In 1961 with the admission of three African American students, Georgia Tech became the first major state university in the Deep South to desegregate without a court order.

In 1968, Whitney M. Young Jr., civil rights leader, spoke at the national convention of the American Institute of Architects (AIA). His speech influenced the Ford Foundation's decision to establish scholarships for African Americans. Seven years later after African Americans entered Georgia Tech as students, the Georgia Tech Afro-American Association (GTAAA) was founded by seventeen African American and white students with the intention of raising student consciousness about race-related issues in 1969, with William J. "Bill" Stanley III, FAIA, B ARCH 1972, as one of the founding members. The group also was to serve as a support group for black students. In 1971, the AIA created a task force on equal opportunity for minority architects to address issues of representation in the profession. Shortly thereafter, a student chapter of the National Organization of Minority Architects (NOMAS) was founded at Georgia Tech.

In 1972, William J. "Bill" Stanley III, FAIA, became the first African American graduate at Georgia Tech to receive the professional Bachelor of Architecture degree. In 1977, his future wife and business partner Ivenue Love-Stanley, FAIA, received the first Bachelor of Architecture degree earned by an African American woman from Georgia Tech and only the twelfth degree awarded to a woman of color in architecture in the United States. She was also the first African American woman to be registered as a licensed architect in the South. Since the founding of their firm in 1978, they have individually and jointly as a firm received numerous awards. His honors include the 1995 Whitney M. Young, Jr. Citation, given by the American Institute of Architects to the country's most socially conscious architect, and in 2000, AIA Georgia bestowed upon him the Bernard Rothschild medal, the state's highest architecture award.

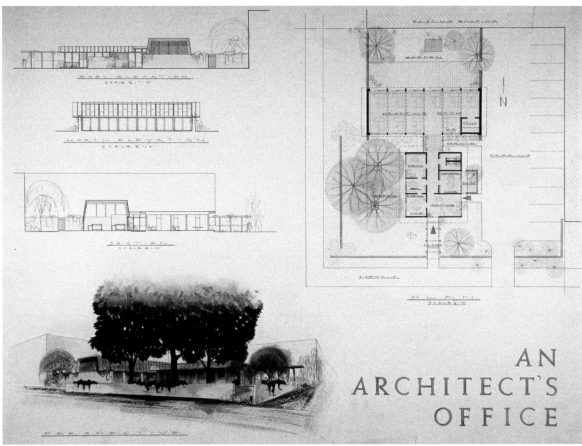

TOP: Kurt Herrman, Jr., *Building Design*
Ink, Watercolor/Board, 30 x 20 inches
Sophomore Design, 1961

BOTTOM: Norman Davenport Askins, *An Architect's Office*
Ink, Watercolor/White Paper, 40 x 30 inches
Sophomore Design, 1963

Arthur Franklin "Frank" Beckum (1926-1990), a native of Wrens, Georgia, was a member of the architecture faculty for thirty-five years. After serving in the Army during World War II, Beckum began his association with Georgia Tech in 1947 as an undergraduate. He obtained both his Bachelor of Science of Architecture (1950) and Bachelor of Architecture (1952) from Georgia Tech. In 1950, he became Tech's first World Student Fund Scholar and studied in Stuttgart, Germany. He later earned a Master of Fine Arts degree from Princeton University. From 1955 until his unanticipated death in 1990, Beckum taught classes in architectural history and design studios. In 1973, Beckum introduced to the teaching of the history survey the concept of the discussion class or preceptorial that he had experienced as a graduate student at Princeton. This tradition continues today. In 1987, he received the ANAK Faculty Award as the distinguished professor at Tech. He served as an Assistant Dean of the College of Architecture from 1982 until his death. The Frank Beckum Memorial Scholarship is awarded each year to a student in his memory.

Joseph N. "Joe" Smith's (1925-2008), architectural studies at Georgia Tech were interrupted by war service during World War II. After serving as a lieutenant with the Navy from 1943 to 1946, Smith returned to complete his studies and receive the four-year Bachelor of Science in Architecture in 1948 and the five-year Bachelor of Architecture in 1949. After graduation Smith returned to his native Florida to practice architecture in Miami, but returned to Atlanta in 1963 to begin a lengthy career with the School of Architecture. Until his retirement from Georgia Tech in 1981, he taught studios, shared his love of watercolor rendering, and served as assistant dean for instruction. During this time, he chaired committees that developed the rationale and administrative organization moving from a School to a College; developed the School's first foreign studies program located originally in Italy that subsequently moved to Paris and is ongoing; developed the planning study for a new architecture building; and developed the three-and-a-half-year Master of Architecture graduate program. After retiring from Georgia Tech, he became a partner with Thompson, Ventulett, Stainback & Associates in charge of the interior design department.

Walter Ennis Parker, Jr., *A World Center for Philosophical Study*
Ink, Watercolor on Board
40 x 30 inches
Senior Design, 1964

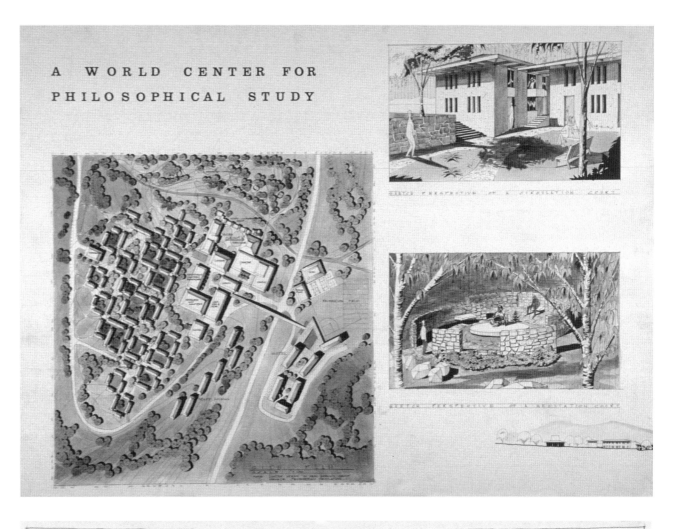

Robert Kirkland
A Garden Center
Ink, Watercolor on White Paper
30 x 20 inches
Fifth Year Design, 1965

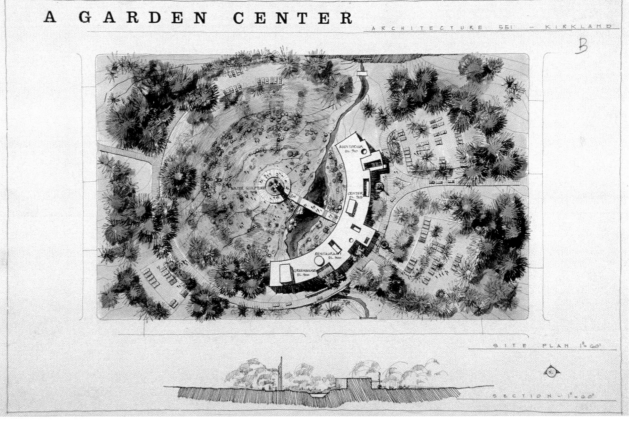

Merrill Elam, AIA, B ARCH 1971, and **Mack Scogin, AIA,** B ARCH 1967, initially worked together at Heery and Heery, Architects and Engineers, Inc. in Atlanta and both gained experience in multidisciplinary architecture and construction design (1969-1981). Scogin and Elam are the sole principals of Mack Scogin Merrill Elam Architects, Inc. and have a twenty-five year legacy of progressive architecture since its founding in 1984. They have individually and jointly received numerous local, regional, and national AIA awards of excellence, including the 1996 Chrysler Award for Innovation in Design and the 2006 Boston Society of Architects Harleston Parker Medal. Their work has also been widely featured in popular and academic publications on architecture and exhibited in many museums and galleries.

Lane M. Duncan received his Bachelor of Architecture from Georgia Tech in 1968, followed by his Masters in Design Studies of Theory and Criticism from Harvard Graduate School of Design in 1987. Duncan has taught from 1975 until his retirement in 2005. He is currently a visiting instructor teaching a visual arts course in watercolor. During his professorship, he has coordinated and taught a wide range of graduate and undergraduate design studios, and also served as graduate thesis advisor and taught many seminars on Theories of Ethics and Aesthetics in Architecture, The Projects and Texts of Louis Kahn, and Serial Painting. Also working in private practice focusing primarily on residential and institutional projects in the southeastern United States, he has acted as design consultant for many national architecture firms.

Elizabeth "Betty" Meredith Dowling received her Bachelor of Architecture from Georgia Tech in 1971 and the Master of Architecture from the University of Illinois in 1972. She began her teaching career in 1973 as a part-time instructor teaching history preceptorials under Professor Frank Beckum. Although she was registered in Georgia as an architect in 1974, she decided to devote her career to teaching architectural history. After receiving her PhD in Architecture from the University of Pennsylvania in 1981, Dowling was hired by Georgia Tech. Now a tenured full professor, she has dedicated more than thirty years to teaching architecture at her alma mater. In addition to her many publications and exhibitions, Dowling founded the Art and Architecture in Greece and Italy summer abroad program.

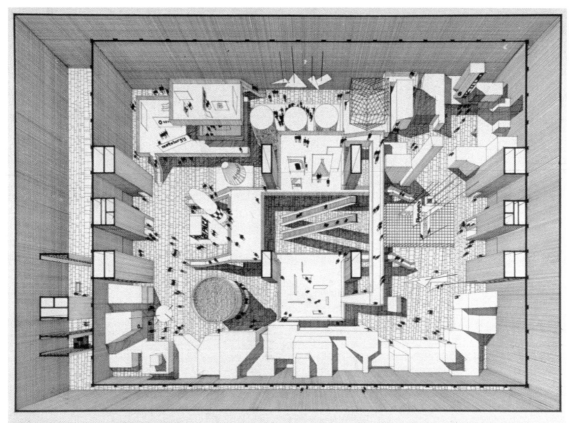

PERSPECTIVE PLAN - ENVIRONMENTAL EXHIBITS

a senate chamber

TOP: Lane M. Duncan, *Technotron*
Ink on Board, 40 x 30 inches
Senior Design, 1968

BOTTOM: John R. Shields, *A Senate Chamber*
Ink, Watercolor on White Paper, 40 x 35.5 inches
Senior Design, 1969

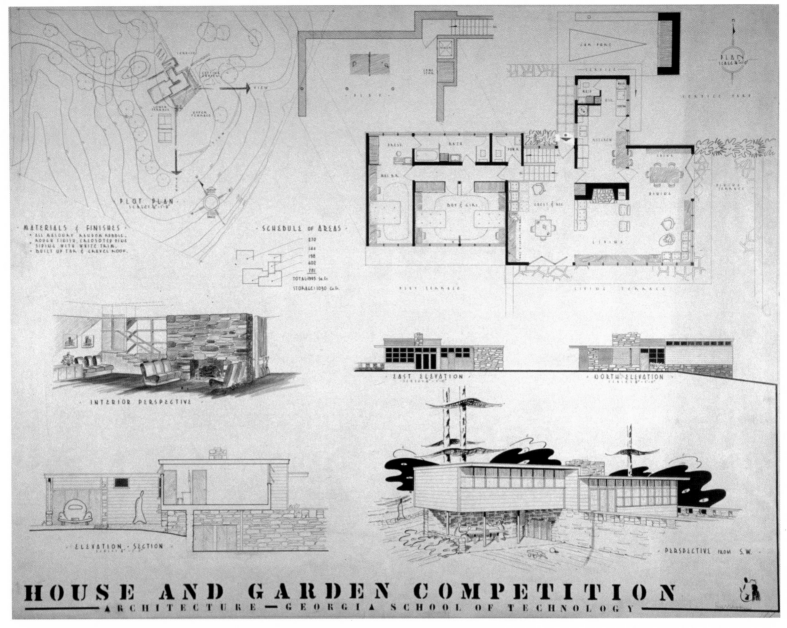

William B. Harrison, *House and Garden Competition*, Ink, Watercolor on White Paper, 40 x 31 inches, 1967

GROWTH AND NEED FOR EXPANSION

Enrollment during the 1950s and early 1960s remained constant, but in the years of 1964 and 1965, there was an increase of incoming freshmen architecture students. In 1966 and 1967, freshman admissions were limited, although transfers from within Georgia Tech kept enrollment stable. The Architecture Building (1952) was designed for 350 students in all four degree programs of architecture, industrial design, building construction, and city planning. However, by 1969, it accommodated as many as 548 students. In the fall of 1970, freshman drawing and graphics classes of architecture were taught in design laboratories of the old Civil Engineering Building and Brown Dormitory. After only eighteen years, the School of Architecture had outgrown its own building; and, only with the practice of intensive use of drafting spaces and careful scheduling, was it able to accommodate the growing needs of the students. Far from ideal conditions, the first and second year students shared drafting tables with as many as three other students.

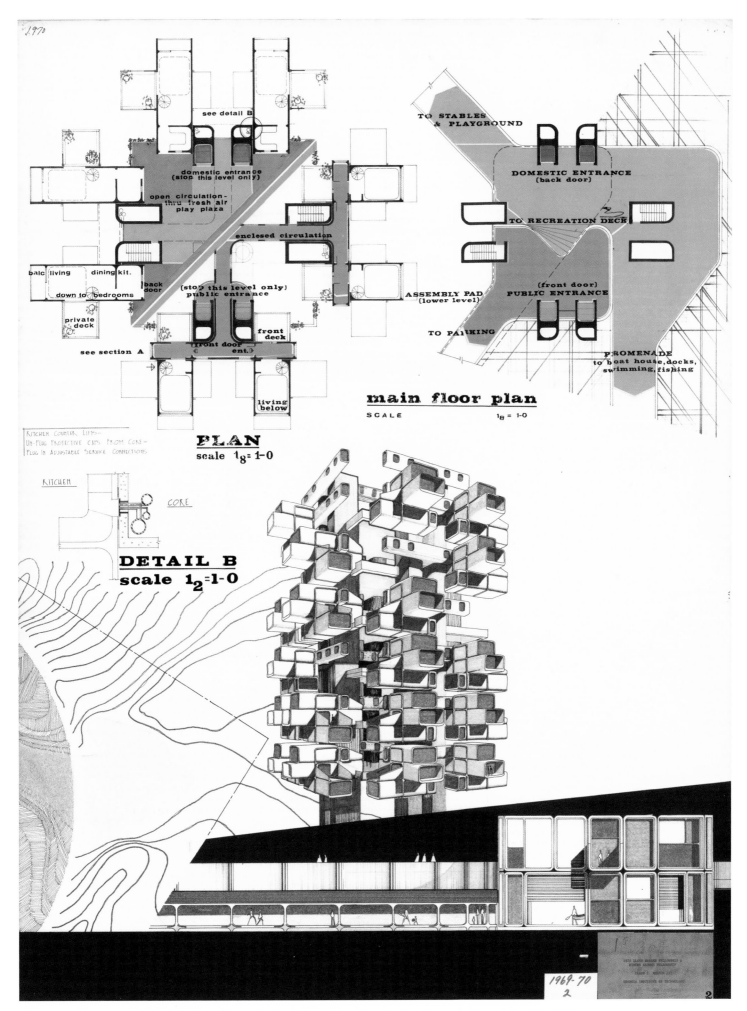

Claud I. Emrich, III, *A Vertical Plug-In Residential Community*, Lloyd Warren Fellowship - 57th Paris Prize in Architecture, First Prize, 1970
Courtesy of Van Alen Institute's Design Competitions Archive

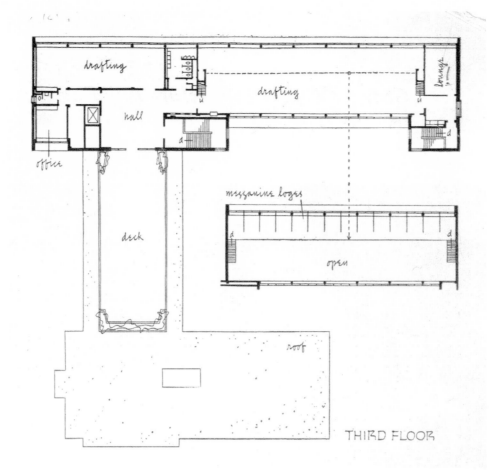

THIRD FLOOR

Fig. 1

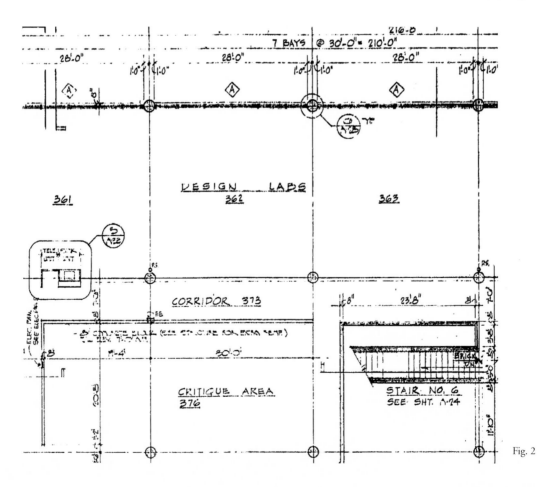

Fig. 2

1973 to Present:
Dialog and Debate

George Barnett Johnston

Recounting history of the recent past is a risky business due in no small measure to the fact that so many of the protagonists, each with their own versions, still survive. So rather than dwelling upon persons and personalities, I begin instead with two plans, both of which should be familiar. The first plan is of the third floor of the east wing of what was once called the School of Architecture. Designed by architects Bush-Brown, Gailey, and Heffernan and completed in 1952, it was published in the journal *Progressive Architecture* in July 1955 (*figure 1*). The second plan is from the set of construction documents for the west wing, the graduate wing, of the College designed by the firm of Cooper Carry Architects and occupied in 1980 (*figure 2*).

Notice in the older plan the notations describing the functions of the spaces. The large open volume, seven bays and more than one hundred feet long, is called out as "drafting"—a drafting room. In the parlance of post-World War II architectural practice, the term "drafting" was becoming increasingly anachronistic as the old divisions between architects and draftsmen perpetuated by habits of class and vocation were giving way to a new emphasis upon design. Note the designation in the adjacent plan of the mezzanine spaces above the drafting room—"loges." This term is a vestige of a romanticized past—the private cubicles in the Beaux-Arts atelier reserved for the focused creativity of the advanced students, while their underlings labored collectively below. Modern for its time in both construction and expression, the notations in this plan reveal nonetheless a building conceived of another era.

Now, comparing the plan of the later addition with the earlier one, a semantic distinction becomes apparent. The third floor drafting spaces in the "old" building are now displaced by "design labs" in the "new" building. The professional transformation from a drafting culture to a design culture has been fully realized. The old hierarchies wherein every architect begins as a draftsman and that maintained the long-hair/short-hair distinction between artistic creation and technical production had given way to some more egalitarian notion demanding simultaneously of all architectural aspirants a new standard of individual creativity and technical acumen. The space of instruction we infer is no longer an atelier where a master must be emulated. Instead, this space is now a laboratory, in deference to the venues devoted to scientific research; however, in this case, the creative process is emphasized rather than scientific method. From drafting as a shaping vocation to design as an impetus for individual expression, the design lab of the 1980 scheme anticipates nonetheless the demands we feel more urgently today for new modes of design research focused on the problems of these challenging times.

This comparison is highly schematic, but it is one meant to crack open assumptions about how architectural education and practice interact in the process of professional formation. As is evident in culture at large, the residue of past practices and ideologies as well as the nascent structures of emergent yet unformulated ones are always and already intertwined in the present. Time and events do not neatly unfold in discreet and logical progressions; rather, this is the order that history imposes in the course of memory lapsing. While the east and west wings *may* be objectified as indices of broader stylistic trends and barometers of technological progress, I propose we consider them instead as built pedagogies, two critics locking horns on a jury, two generations and more of architectural professors and students, each anticipating and critiquing the other, both propagators and products of the professional conflicts we confront today.

In the interval of time between the completion of the east wing and the construction of the west wing, architectural education and practice, both nationally and locally, underwent startling challenges and changes. In the late sixties and early seventies, the School of Architecture at Georgia Tech, then organized around a five-year Bachelor of Architecture program, came under withering criticism from the National Architectural Accrediting Board. In 1966, the accreditation team reported, "The School seems to be dangerously lacking in dynamism, in self-renewal, and in a spirit of innovation. It is still basking, as it were, in the stability established during the long leadership of the previous director."[1] National studies on architectural education and practice, among them the influential "Princeton Report" of 1967 commissioned by the American Institute of Architects (AIA), called for sweeping reforms in education for environmental design to meet the challenges of the time: exploding information and the specialization of tasks within an increasingly complex design and building enterprise. In the early seventies, the self-regulating autonomy of the profession itself was challenged as the U.S. Department of Justice held elements of the AIA's Code of Ethics limiting professional advertising and competition by fee to be in violation of the Sherman Anti-Trust Act. Meanwhile, the rational basis of modern architecture was being challenged by monumental urban crises in which urban renewal had become as pernicious as urban decay. The demolition of the infamous Pruitt-Igoe housing project in St. Louis heralded for some the death of modern architecture itself. Complexity and contradiction, indeed!

In 1973, the five-year professional curriculum at Georgia Tech gave way to a four-year undergraduate and a two-year graduate program leading to the Master of Architecture professional degree. The old School of Architecture under the College of Engineering became the stand-alone, multidisciplinary College of Architecture in 1975; and its first dean, William L. Fash, soon made a number of strategic hires that set the College on a course of research and scholarship for the renewal of disciplinary and professional education. To accommodate this new mission and to house an expanding population of students, faculty, and research programs, the graduate wing of the College was completed in 1980.

By all accounts, the process for the design of the addition of the west wing yielded many raw emotions—a resigned commission, a substitute choice, derogatory comparisons. The project was described in print as "hard-edged,"[2] but also by a visiting accreditation team as a "fine [example] of the architecture of its time" worthy of respect for the "formal and ideological values implicit in the building."[3] It is a corduroy building compared to the bowtie and tweed jacket next door. It is the west wing to the east wing, left wing to the right wing. Internal spatial boundaries are implicit, fluid, contestable, negotiable—a liberal, participatory democracy. It is a didactic building meant, according to architect Jerry Cooper, to "hit you on the back of head" with its anatomical lessons of structure, enclosure, and systems.[4] It is a moody building, somber on gray days yet susceptible to surprising bouts of weightlessness and laughter in light. It is a tough building, challenging everyone who works in it to "go ahead, make my day." And at the same time, it is a background building, a stage that yields the spotlight to all coming attractions. Whatever its strengths or flaws, the true proof of the building has been the creative spirits that it set spinning inside.

In 1985, controversy swirled around the public judging by invited critics of the SGF Competition, an in-house challenge-to-excellence and design free-for-all endowed by patron Herb Cohen in 1974.[5] According to the *Atlanta Constitution*'s arts and architecture reporter Catherine Fox, "passions flared and jurors and students [came] to verbal blows." Fox goes on to note:

> The controversy began during the preliminary jurying of the projects of seven different studios. The professor for each studio determines its theme, and this year the subjects included both conventional architectural problems and theoretical ones. Some students designed specific buildings, while others made objects that related to their study of literature and non-specific architectural issues.
>
> . . . [T]he controversy erupted when a jury led by New York architect Raimond Abraham refused to even critique one of these theoretical studios on the grounds that the resulting projects . . . were not architecture. . . .
>
> The students from the rejected studio . . . issued a statement castigating the jury for its inflexibility, which occasioned prolonged applause from the students. Abraham . . . promptly resigned the jury and left the campus.
>
> The issue did not die. Two projects from another theoretical studio prompted more debate. Peter Chermayeff, an architect from Cambridge, Mass. was willing to admire the students' projects as objects but considered them invalid as architecture and criticized the school for even holding such studios at all. Mack Scogin, an Atlanta architect, defended the projects as a means of stimulating the creative process and personal probing that precedes making actual buildings.
>
> Ironically, both the first and third prizes were awarded to students who participated in the non-building studios. Bruce Fabrick won first place for a meditation on the lives of a city that took the form of a tall, narrow

Fig. 3

Fig. 5

Fig. 4

Figure 1. Bush-Brown, Gailey, and Heffernan Architects. Third floor plan, Georgia Tech School of Architecture. From *Progressive Architecture*, July 1955.

Figure 2. Cooper Carry Architects. Third floor plan, Georgia Tech College of Architecture. Construction drawings, 1978.

Figure 3. Bruce Fabrick. First Prize, 1985 SGF Competition. Detail of plaster cast.

Figure 4. Bruce Fabrick. First Prize, 1985 SGF Competition. Chest of drawers containing plaster casts.

Figure 5. Cooper Carry Architects. Interior at east entry, Georgia Tech College of Architecture.

chest, which contained a plaster impression of "remains" or urban fossils in each of its drawers or archaeological layers. A lengthy text and several drawings accompanied the chest.[6]

Fabrick's project was not retained in the College's archives, but rather languishes, with poetic virtue intact, in the basement of his home—a reminder that the historical record, as his project archaeologically suggests, is full of gaps, schisms, elisions, and omissions (*figures 3 and 4*).

Not controversy for controversy's sake, mind you—though some may have seen it as so. The aftershocks of that event had ramifications then, and they still reverberate in the echo chamber of the west wing atrium. Esoteric things and, with equal valence and validity, makerly material things became the focus of graduate theses and masters projects. Critical and sometimes self-indulgent approaches to problems of expression and representation were intertwined with urban speculations and critiques of speculative development. In some senses, the Architecture Program turned inward for a time. A fellowship of students with a charismatic teacher inserted a powerful presence into the atrium, materializing through long and labored efforts the poetic power of architecture in the realization of architect John Hejduk's allegorical *House of Suicide* and *House of the Mother of Suicide*. The sublime tension between those objects and their setting, sometimes as if buried in a concrete cave, other times shaded under a concrete tent, sacralized the school's introspection. A whole host of other students and faculty pointed us outward, however, and took on the city of Atlanta and its problems through direct action and intervention. Mad Housers,[7] impatient with bureaucratic excuses for doing so little about homelessness took matters into their own hands in the provision of primitive huts to those lacking basic shelter. An insurgency of one in the form of a self-styled architectural jihadist waged aesthetic holy war against the wholesale destruction of Atlanta's architectural legacy. Scrutinizing the evidence at hand, another engaged and insightful student saw the possibility of transforming Atlanta through the development of an abandoned transportation corridor, a beltline cinching the urban core.

As the students' passionate engagement changed the Program, so too did the era's progressive politics begin to transform the composition of the students' ranks. Over the course of the decades since 1978 when Georgia Tech began to systematically record such statistics, we can see a dramatic shift in the character and complexion of the student body. Within the College, steady gains in the proportional enrollment of female students has brought us to near gender parity, this within an institute where overall female enrollment remains less than thirty percent. The situation within the Architecture Program is even more impressive, and within some graduate classes, the old balance is actually reversed. Reflective, however, of a professional legacy of inequality, gender balance among full-time faculty of the College still lags behind the student body. But the conventional wisdom and social closure that once defined the profession of architecture as both white and male is surely eroding if current trends within this College bear out across the nation. In the Architecture Program, white male students comprise a distinct minority as compared to all other groups; though again, among the professoriate of the College, the situation remains the inverse. Today, the all-male drafting wing restrooms in the 1952 building have mostly been converted. In the 1980 addition, the male-female plumbing duality was thoroughly embedded in the design, though with unnerving floor-to-floor reversals that still baffle and surprise.

The broad scattershot of creativity that defined the SGF Competition at its peak as the lifeblood of the program was dissipated long before the competition was discontinued. The Ventulett Chair in Architecture now serves some of that role, though in a more sober way, through the design and research agendas of distinguished faculty members. Other models of multidisciplinary and team-based design research, such as the Solar Decathlon project, also motivate imagination and problem solving. It is intriguing to observe these installations and interrogations—much concerned with matters of digital fabrication and mass customization—posed within, upon, and juxtaposed to the concrete tectonic fabric of the Cooper Carry addition. Whether parasitic or paratactic constructions, they criticize the building, but they are enveloped and absorbed by it as well. Old questions of structure and ornament, decoration and construction, still come to the fore. Is the west wing more Greek or Gothic: a constructed ornament or else a core-form, a rational structure stripped bare, awaiting the return of an ornamental motive?

This is a partial story of recent times, a temporal "joint" in the history of architectural education at Georgia Tech, but it holds a certain analogy with the expansion joint that physically connects the east and west wings. It is a troublesome connection; it has bothered me now for twenty-five years. Is it an affront to the old building or a sloppy kiss? I understand its technical necessity, the need to pull back the column, cantilever over and avoid the old building's foundation—to tie the buildings together, to hold them apart. Yet the original presentation model clearly shows the new construction to be subordinate to the old. The end result, however, is quite the opposite. There must be a story in that joint, one I am unable to adequately account for in this space.

By shifting gazes from the construction drawings to the constructed effects, however, one finds in the building a series of virtual joints that are supplemental and perhaps compensatory to that more problematical connection. The expanse of glass on the east face forms an aperture, a mirror, a lens for more subtle exchanges. By daylight, through intense reflection, the brick surface of the old building's bridge connector is projected onto the lobby floor of the new, to be trod across as if a welcome mat; by night, the concrete addition projects its atrium space outward into the darkness, and the stair that descends inside the west wing appears to ascend through the courtyard and mount back up to the other side (*figure 5*). The two buildings are engaged in an ongoing dialog and debate, like two critics locking horns, agreeing to disagree on some things, and then reminiscing and maybe gossiping over drinks.

—George Barnett Johnston, PhD, is an Associate Professor of Architecture at Georgia Tech.

NOTES

1. National Architectural Accrediting Board Visiting Team Report (April 21, 1966).

2. Robert Adams Ivy, "'Preparing Architects to Question and Explore': Georgia Tech School of Architecture, Atlanta," Architecture: *The AIA Journal* 77, no. 8 (1988): 74-77.

3. National Architectural Accrediting Board Visiting Team Report (July 9, 1997): 23.

4. Jerry Cooper, in conversation with the author, February 12, 2009.

5. The so-called SGF Competition was named for Cohen's company, the Southern GF Company.

6. Catherine Fox, "Controversy Builds in Architectural Competition," *Atlanta Constitution*, December 9, 1985, sec. B.

7. A small group of architecture students who called themselves Mad Housers built free shelter for Atlanta's homeless with the idea that a secure and stable place to live can enable and empower people to find other resources to help themselves.

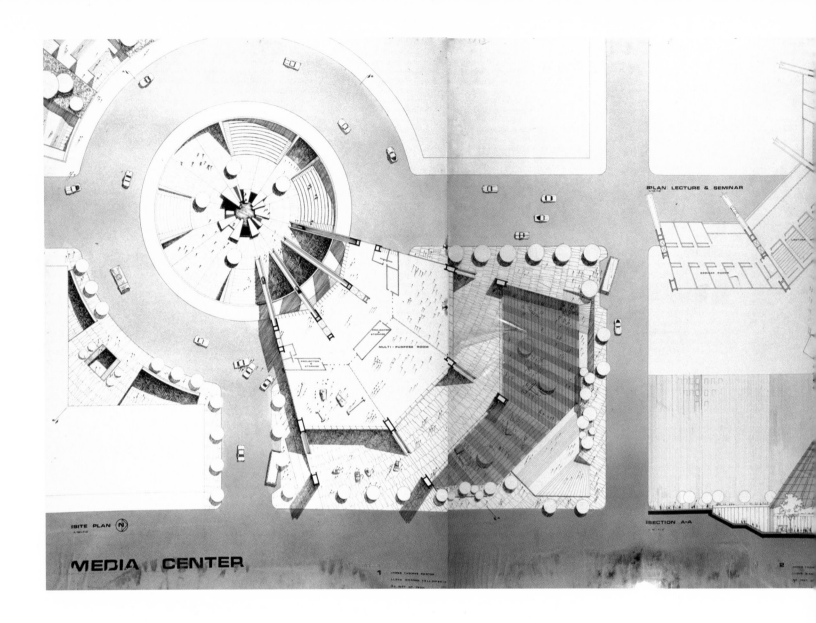

INITIATION OF GRADUATE EDUCATION

Profound changes awaited the Architecture Program in the 1970s, including a new curriculum, a new status as a college, significant expansion of the faculty, and a major building addition. These changes marked a major shift in the self-conception of the faculty and administration. As noted in the critical remarks of the National Architectural Accrediting Board (NAAB) report of April 21, 1966:

> The School seems to be dangerously lacking in dynamism, in self-renewal, and in a sprit of innovation. It is still basking, as it were, in the stability established during the long leadership of the previous director. More than half the faculty survive from a period that ended a decade ago. Several of these faculty members seem quite content to continue indefinitely at a low rank even though there is patently no room for them at the top. Little curricular innovation seems to have been introduced since the spin-off of industrial design and city planning much earlier.

In the subsequent NAAB review letter of May 26, 1971, addressed to Georgia Tech President Arthur G. Hansen, continuing concerns are noted alongside faint praise and encouragement to reorganize the curriculum to address future needs of the profession. In response to the program's stated purpose "to put professional students into their respective fields with a superior background of general studies and a broad experience in related professional studies," the NAAB responded with "the School is highly professionally oriented and is delivering a good product within this framework. The objectives of a distinguished school, however, cannot be stated in terms of delivering a product." The reviewers restricted the program accreditation to three years rather than the standard five-year accreditation. Commenting on the curriculum structure, they noted:

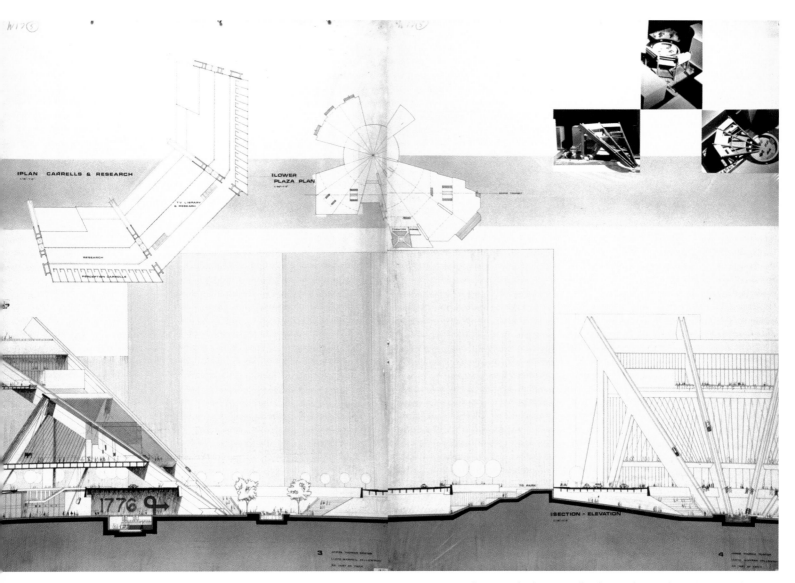

James Thomas Porter, *Media Center,* Lloyd Warren Fellowship - 59th Annual Paris Prize in Architecture,
First Alternate Ink, Airbrush, Photos on Board, 30 x 40 inches, Boards 1, 2, 3, and 4 of 5, Fifth Year Design, 1972

The present structure of the School is a five-year degree in Architecture. This is the program which emerged during the 1930s and is being phased out by most of the leading Schools of Architecture and Planning throughout the United States. The desirability of moving into a six-year program with concentrations in the areas which can be supported through related disciplines on the campus of Georgia Tech is obvious. It is the conviction of the Visiting Committee that the School should seriously consider moving to the 4+2 year program.

Although a faculty curriculum committee had studied the concept of moving to this new program for three years, the NAAB report spurred action. In the following year in response to this critical NAAB report, the committee chaired by Professor Arnall T. "Pat" Connell and Joseph N. "Joe" Smith produced a detailed proposal to phase out the five-year Bachelor of Architecture degree and replace it with a four-year undesignated Bachelor of Science and a two-year Master of Architecture. The faculty report cited the reasons for the change were "to develop a curriculum and associated degree structure that will better prepare architects to serve society within the framework of a changing profession and that will enable the school to contribute to the creation of knowledge needed for the development of a better designed physical environment." The new curriculum was a first step in remaking the professional conception of the then sixty-five-year-old school. With the new vision as a graduate school, additional supporting decisions followed including administrative reorganization as the College of Architecture in 1975 and new faculty hires that were capable of delivering a progressive graduate education.

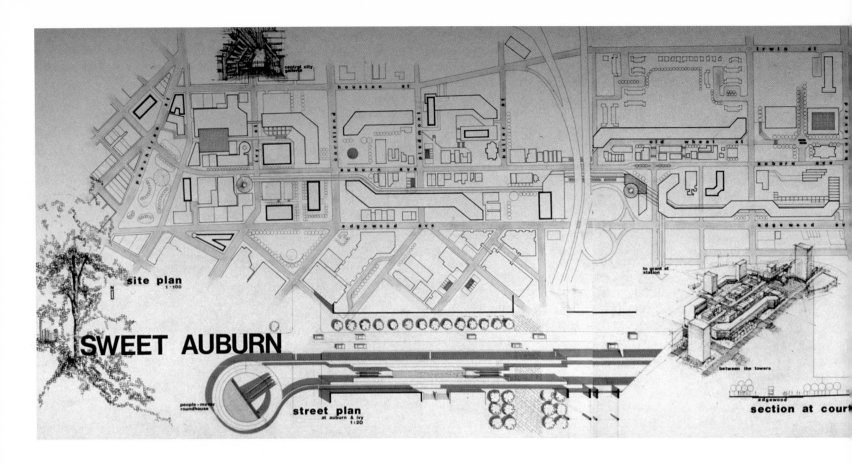

SGF PRIZE

Begun in 1974, the SGF Prize was one of the most significant in-house juried design competition in the one-hundred-year history of the Architecture Program. Named for the Southern GF Company and its president Herbert B. Cohen, the SGF Prize began as an advanced student competition with a commitment of five years. The program grew in significance to the intellectual life of the graduate program and survived until the final competition was held in 2008. The initial prize included not only a monetary stipend for travel-study but also a small bronze statue by famed Italian sculptor Arnaldo Pomodoro. The conceptual framework of the competition encouraged experimental design exploration and the funding provided the opportunity for students to learn from the comments of jurists of international reputation.

The first recipient of the SGF Prize was Charles H. Albright, B ARCH 1974. Although his winning project was not retained, the 1975 project of winner John S. Abbott Jr., B ARCH 1975, is pictured above. The thirty-fifth award in 2008 marked the termination of the SGF Prize with the winning entry submitted by Anthony Piede, BS ARCH 2006, M ARCH 2008.

In addition to Georgia Tech professors, the first SGF jury included local architects Jerome M. Cooper, BS ARCH 1952, B ARCH 1955, jury chair, Edward H. Shirley, and Thomas W. Ventulett, III, B ARCH 1957, with invited external critic Pershing Wong, B ARCH 1951, with I.M. Pei & Partners, New York, who served on the jury yearly through 1980.

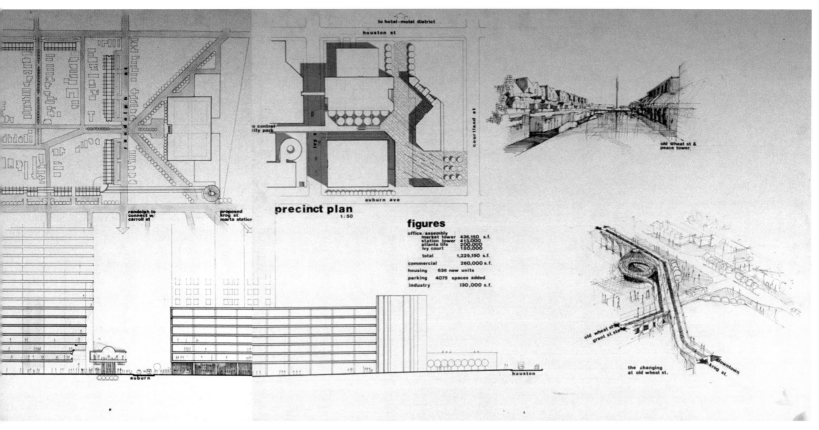

John S. Abbot, *Sweet Auburn*, SGF Competition, First Prize,
Ink, Airbrush, Photos on Boards, 40 x 30 inches, Boards 1, 2, and 3 of 4, Fifth Year Design, 1975

Subsequent juries included notable architects, writers, and critics including:

Merrill Elam; Mack Scogin; Stanley Abercrombie, senior editor of *The AIA Journal*;

George Hartman, Hartman & Cox, Washington, D.C.; Philip Babb, Richard Meier & Partners, New York;

Peter Eisenman, Eisenman/Robertson Architects, New York; Peter Davey, editor, *Architectural Review*, London;

Fred Koetter, Koetter/Kim & Associates, Boston; Peter Chermayeff Cambridge 7, Cambridge, Massachusetts;

Raimond Abraham, The Cooper Union, New York; Michael Sorkin, architectural critic, *Village Voice*;

Robert McAnulty, Robertson + McAnulty, Architects, New York; Jeffrey Kipnis, Cooper Union;

Mario Gandelsonas, Yale University; Lauretta Vinciarelli, Columbia University; Tony Vidler, Princeton University;

Thom Mayne, Morphosis, Santa Monica, California; Steven M. Holl, New York; Eric Owen Moss, Culver City, California;

Peter Walker, San Francisco; Diana Agrest, Agrest and Gandelsonas, Architects, New York

PARIS PROGRAM

In 1972, Professor Joseph N. "Joe" Smith, III received support for his concept of creating a year-long academic program in Europe that ultimately became what is now known as the Paris Program. The budding venture began as a summer program in the University of Georgia facilities in Cortona, Italy, where it remained for two years. He was assisted there by Italian architect Dr. Sergio Lenci, who later helped him move the program to Rome in its third year. The goal of finding a permanent home in a major European city for an expanded full-year program was achieved in 1975. Jose Charlet and M. Bertin, director of the Ecole des Beaux-Arts in Paris, made an attractive proposal that was accepted to select the Unite Pedagogique d'Architecture 7 as the home for the year-long academic program in architecture. These professors were known personally by former architecture director P. M. Heffernan from his student years at the Ecole.

The director for the initial year was Associate Professor George Ramsey, a recipient of the Diplôme Par Le Gouvernement (DPLG). Instruction took place inside temporary classroom trailers set within the yet-to-be-restored grandeur of the iron-and-glass Grand Palais built for the 1900 World's Fair. The first group included thirty-nine fourth-year students, with quarterly instruction by Professors Pat Connell, John Kelly, and Robert Segrest. In the second year, eighteen students were instructed by Lane Duncan, P. M. Heffernan, John Kelly, and Dale Durfee. Since the initiation of the program, it has been directed by Professors Robert Craig, Cheryl Morgan, Robert Bridges, Lewis Lanter, and Elliott Pavlos. Since 1995, Professor Libero Andreotti, BS 1980, M ARCH 1982, has both taught and directed the program. The staff has grown from a single director and visiting Georgia Tech faculty to include Professor Marc Bedarida, instructors Xavier Wrona and Damien Valero, and administrator and language instructor Anja Valero. After several years in the Grand Palais, the program relocated to Tolbiac. In 1994, following a reorganization of the French teaching system, the program relocated again to the Ecole Nationale Supérieure d'Architecture de Paris La Villette (one of the eight remaining successor schools of the Ecole des Beaux-Arts, and one of only three remaining within the city of Paris). Since the founding of the Paris Program, more than 750 students have completed their undergraduate design education in the environment of one of Europe's most significant centers of design.

First Full Year Class
Paris Program, 1975-1976

OPPOSITE: Peter John Polites, *A Consciousness Center*
Lloyd Warren Fellowship - 59th Annual Paris Prize in Architecture
Honorable Mention, Ink on Board, 30 x 40 inches
Board 1 of 5, Fifth Year Design, 1972

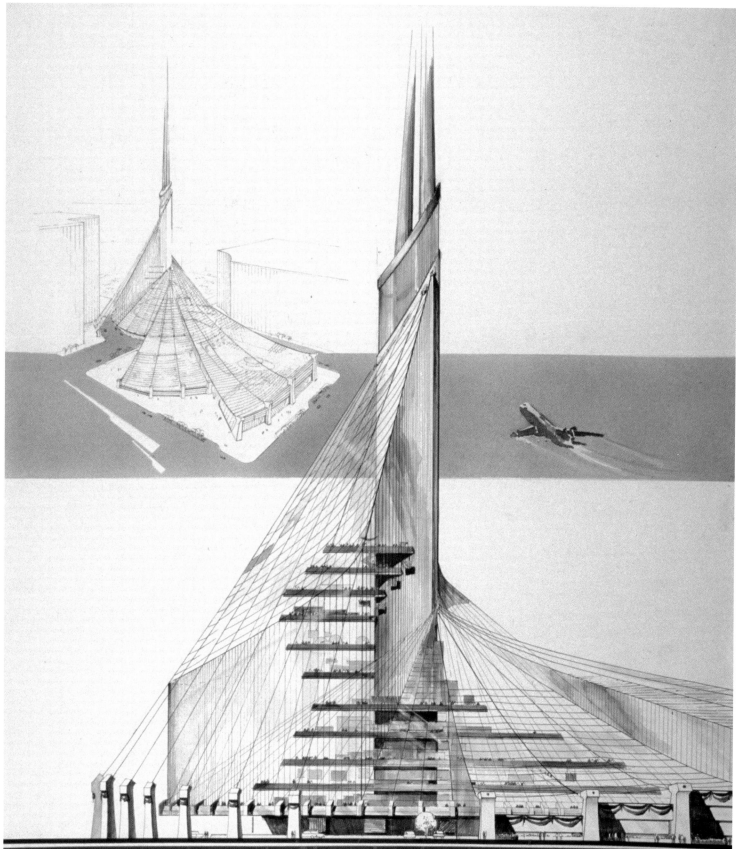

ELEVATION

59th PARIS PRIZE – A CON

William L. Ruark, Jr., *Fish on Stairs*, Airbrush, Watercolor on Board, Visual Communications Studio, 1985

FREEHAND DRAWING

Until the advent of computer drafting, and with it the developing techniques in computer modeling, freehand drawing served as a fundamental skill in the architectural curriculum. From the first classes in 1908, the skills of pencil and ink rendering, live-model sketching, and watercolor were essential to expressing three-dimensional concepts by two-dimensional means. As evidenced by the student work, interest in rendering never even diminished during the transformation from the Beaux-Arts to the Bauhaus system. In the 1970s, the courses were termed "visual communications" and the staff grew to include no fewer than three professors at any time. Among the artists providing instruction in the art of drawing and rendering were Julian Harris, George Beattie, John Hardy, Albert Smith, Whit Connah, and Joan Templer. Additional instruction was provided in black-and-white photography. Watercolor rendering and photography are the remaining arts that continue to be offered in the current curriculum.

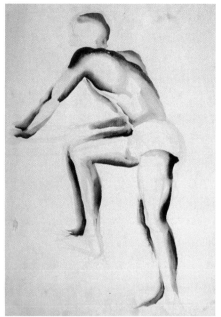

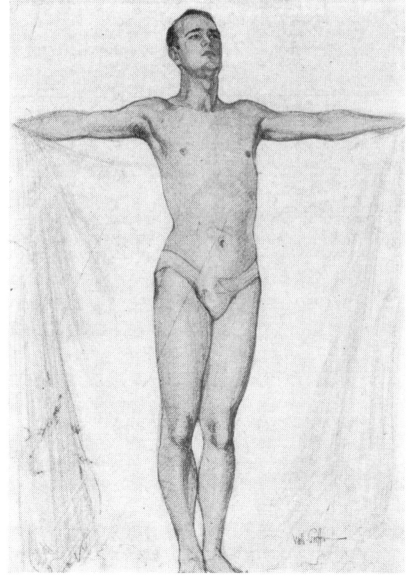

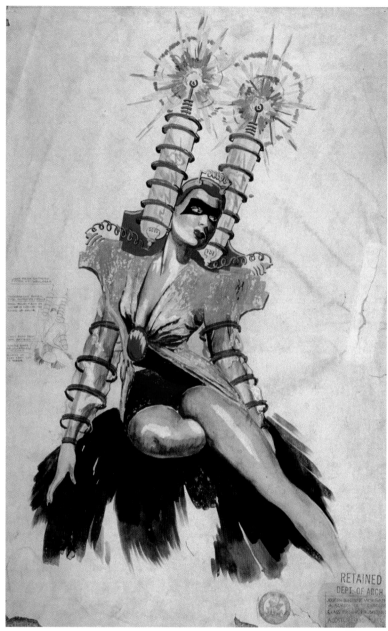

ABOVE: Joseph Warner Morgan, *A Costume and Mask*
Watercolor on White paper; 20 x 30.5 inches, 1940

LEFT, TOP: Carol Mosman Smith, Life Drawing, 1930

LEFT, BOTTOM: Will Griffin, Life Drawing, 1926

In 1976, William L. "Bill" Fash (1931-2002) became the first dean of the College of Architecture. Fash came to Tech from the University of Illinois, where he served as a professor of architecture and director of the graduate program. Prior to his tenure at Illinois, he held teaching positions at the University of Oregon and Oklahoma State University, where he earned his bachelor's degree in architecture in 1958 and his Master of Architecture in 1960. He also received a Fulbright Scholarship while at Oklahoma State.

The influence of his leadership was immediately felt with the College of Architecture assuming an intellectual character that placed it on a more equal footing with the larger and more established colleges on campus. Within Fash's first six years as dean, the College celebrated a new building, the addition of a doctoral program, and a growing research agenda by individual faculty that culminated into the creation of major research centers. The Center for Rehabilitation Technology (founded 1980), now the Center for Assistive Technology and Environmental Access) and the Construction Resource Center (founded 1987) became the first two research centers within the College.

In the late 1970s, the College of Architecture initiated a program of study leading to the Doctor of Philosophy degree in Architecture. Through the leadership of John Templer, the doctoral program's first director, the intellectual scope of the College broadened with advanced study, interdisciplinary research, and scholarship in architecture and city planning. In 1982, Georgia Tech and the Board of Regents approved the doctoral degree program in architecture, initiated by Fash.

In addition, Fash implemented an array of research arenas within the professional degree, focusing on building design and performance. As the research program continued to grow in magnitude and capabilities, new proposals were made and grants awarded. A fairly new branch of the College, the research program was gaining national recognition and esteem, as evidenced by its acceptance of the Human Environment Award in 1982 presented by the American Society of Interior Designers.

John A. Kelly achieved the designation of Professor Emeritus following thirty-five years of service to the program and College of Architecture. Kelly began teaching in the Architecture Program in 1963 immediately after receiving his bachelor's degree in architecture from Oklahoma State University. Taking a leave of absence from teaching, he travelled in Europe after winning the 1964 Lloyd Warren Fellowship - Annual Paris Prize in Architecture. Kelly pursued further academic studies and received a Master of Architectural Engineering from Oklahoma State in 1967 and a Master of Architecture from the University of Illinois in 1968. After returning to Georgia Tech, Kelly taught all levels of design studio, structural theory, architectural graphics, and visual communications. His career included significant administrative positions as associate dean (1983-1993) and director of the Architecture Program (1996-2000). Kelly retired in 2000 from Georgia Tech to continue private practice in architecture and interior design work with his firm Kelly + Associates.

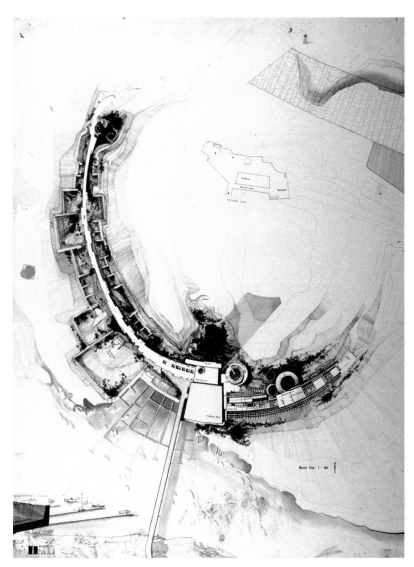

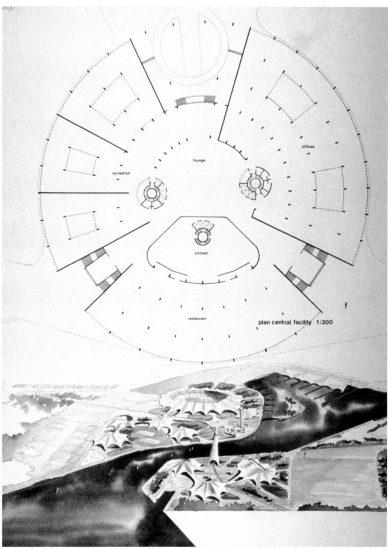

John J. Rossini, *A World Ecology*
William Van Alen Architect Memorial Fellowship,
Second Annual International Competition, Second Prize
Ink, Pencil, Watercolor on Board, 30 x 40 inches
Board 1 of 3, Fifth Year Design, 1973

Steven R. Groves, *Olympic Games Complex*
William Van Alen Architect Memorial Fellowship
Third Annual International Competition
Ink, Watercolor on Board, 30 x 40 inches
Board 2 of 5, 1974

Dale Alden Durfee, AIA (1944-2006) energized the design studios upon his arrival in 1966. He had recently completed his architectural educaton with an undergraduate degree from Oklahoma State University and a Masters degree in architecture from the University of Illinois at Urbana-Champaign. His expertise in watercolor developed the rendering technique of many of his students in this media making it a hallmark of Georgia Tech competition entries for decades. His high-rise studio trained a generation of future architects who employed their knowledge in creating the urban centers of many American cities. In addition to teaching he also operated an award winning design firm from 1966 to 2004 that received nurmerous recognitions including six on the national or international levels. In 1999 he was selected as the college's Outstanding Professor. He retired from teaching in 2000 and was conferred the honor of Professor Emeritus in 2001.

Robert M. Craig, PhD

In the process of change to a 4+2 program that emphasized graduate education, Professor Robert M. "Rob" Craig was the first of the new hires. With a Bachelor of Arts degree in history and education from Principia College (1966); a Master of Arts degree in history from the University of Illinois (1967); and a doctorate in the history of architecture and urban development from Cornell University (1973), Craig demonstrated the new academic direction the future College of Architecture would follow. Focusing on nineteenth- and early twentieth-century architecture with a concentration in American, modern, and medieval architecture, Rob created new courses on Frank Lloyd Wright, the arts and crafts, Atlanta architecture, architecture of the United States, and medieval architecture. He also devoted enormous energy to the development of new professional organizations such as the Southeast Chapter of the Society of Architectural Historians (SESAH) that was founded at Georgia Tech in 1981. He has served as the president of the Southeast American Society for Eighteenth-Century Studies and the Nineteenth-Century Studies Association, and as the secretary of the national Society of Architectural Historians. He has written numerous essays and journal articles. His most recent book is *Bernard Maybeck at Principia College: The Art & Craft of Building* (2004), which received the SESAH Book Award in 2005.

Douglas C. Allen, ASLA

Senior Associate Dean and Professor Douglas C. Allen, ASLA, received his academic training in landscape architecture at the University of Georgia and Harvard University. Allen joined the faculty in 1977 as one of the first hires aimed at expanding the graduate curriculum of the Architecture Program with its professional two-year Master of Architecture degree. He broadened the understanding of connections between urban design and architecture through his course History of Urban Form and also through his teaching in the College of Architecture's summer program in Italy beginning in 1994. His professional career has been recognized through numerous design awards of excellence, including ones given by the Urban Land Institute, the National AIA, the Southeast Region AIA, the Georgia Chapter of the AIA, and the Atlanta Urban Design Commission. In recognition of his outstanding teaching, Allen received the 2006 ANAK Faculty Award.

THE LOUVRE

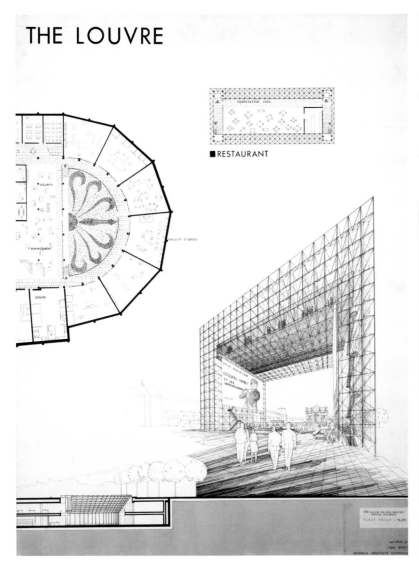

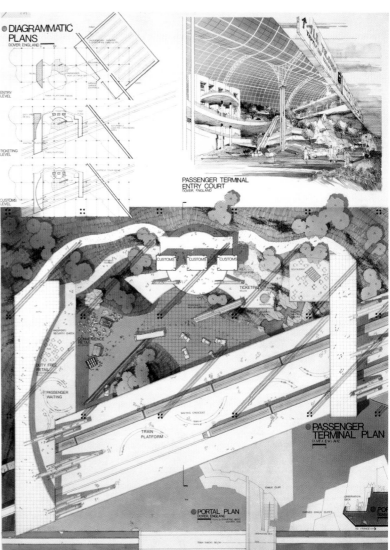

Tom Spector, *An Audio-Visual Center for a Great Museum: The Louvre*
William Van Alen Architect Memorial Fellowship, Ninth Annual International Competition
First Prize, Pen and Ink, 40 x 30 inches, Board 4 of 4, Second Year Graduate Studio, 1980
Courtesy of Van Alen Institute's Design Competitions Archive

James B. Wauford, *English Channel Tunnel: The Approaches from Dover and Calais*
William Van Alen Architect Memorial Fellowship, Tenth Annual International Competition
First Prize, Ink, Watercolor, 40 x 30 inches, Board 1 of 4, Second Year Graduate Studio
Studio Critic John Kelly, 1981, Courtesy of Van Alen Institute's Design Competitions Archive

Richard W. Fredlund, *NIAE Street Fair*, NIAE Student Design Competition, First Prize
Ink, Color, Airbrush, 30 x 40 inches, Sixth Year Design, 1977

Richard Dagenhart, AIA

Richard Dagenhart also was hired in 1977 to further strengthen the graduate program in the realm of urban design. His own graduate training at the University of Pennsylvania with master's degrees in architecture and city planning occurred during the inspirational tenure of Louis I. Kahn. Now a full-time associate professor of architecture and adjunct professor of city and regional planning, Dagenhart has taught architectural and urban design studios, as well as lectured and led fundamental course seminars in urban design theory and practice. As an architect and a fellow of the Institute for Urban Design, he has augmented his academic career at Georgia Tech with his continually developing professional practice in architecture and urban design in Philadelphia, Houston, and Atlanta. His award-winning projects include downtown urban design projects, planning, urban design for historic districts, and urban housing design.

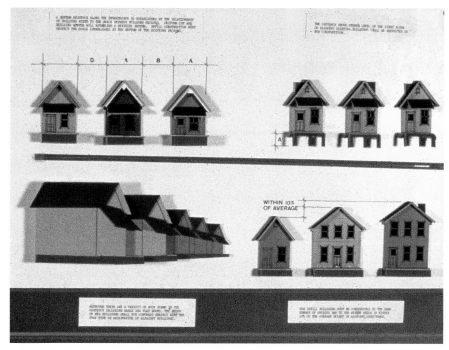

Steve Cover/John Tuggle, Jr., *Cabbagetown Historic District Guidelines*
SGF Prize, First Place, Posterboard/Chipboard Bas Relief, 30 x 40 inches, Boards 2 and 3 of 3
Second Year Graduate Studio, Studio Critic Richard Dagenhart, 1981

Alan Balfour

In 1977, Alan Balfour came to the attention of the Architecture Program director search committee due to his impressive history of research at the Massachusetts Institute of Technology, where he had received $350,000 from the Andrew W. Mellon Foundation to develop a stronger understanding of the character and the significance of architectural education. The resulting study was published in 1981 in two volumes as the Architectural Education Study. From September 1978 to June 1988, Balfour served as professor and director of programs in Architecture. During this period, he strengthened the Master of Architecture program and added a written and a design thesis requirement, resulting in an impressive body of research by master's students. In 1987, Balfour created the first graduate-level summer study abroad program in London. He arranged for the students to meet well-known figures and others who would soon prove to be avant-garde leaders in architecture. Invited lecturers included Alvin Boyarsky, Zaha Hadid, Quinlan Terry, Micha Bandini, Rem Koolhaas, and Peter Cook. In 2008, Balfour would return to the College as dean.

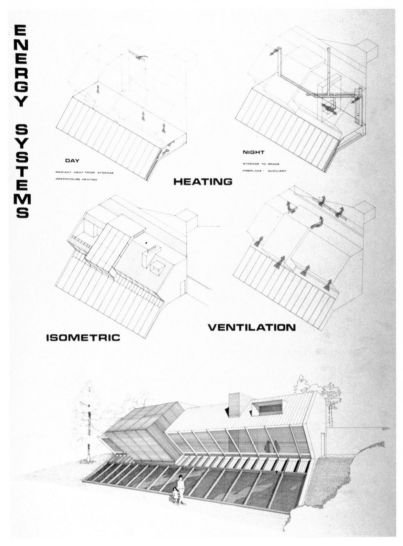

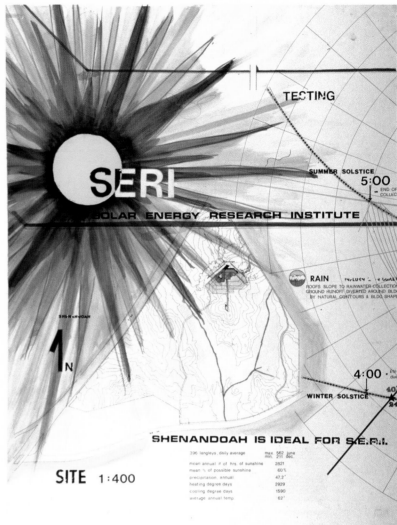

John Adams, *Solar Dwelling*, Ink on Board, 30 x 40 inches
Board 3 of 3, Junior Design, 1975

Author Unidentified, *Solar Energy Research Institute*, 1979

SOCIAL AND ENVIRONMENTAL AWARENESS

Concern for the environment reached a wider audience with the initiation of Earth Day in 1969. Sustainable design slowly grew over the decades from the concern of a minority of professors like George Ramsey to the status of serious academic issues requiring independent coursework and studio focus. The 2007 Solar Decathlon Project substantiates the current level of interest.

In 1980 the Center for Rehabilitation Technology became the first research center in the College. Now named Center for Assistive Technology and Environmental Access (CATEA), it is one of the College's seven research centers. The *Chronical of Higher Education* released its 2007 national rankings of faculty production in research univerisites placing the Georgia Tech College of Architecture at number three for the category of architecture.

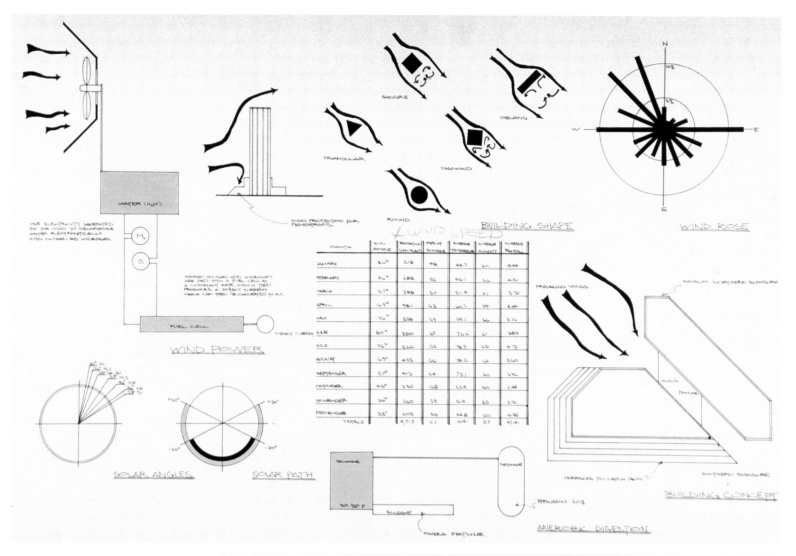

ABOVE:
Steve Keller, *Solar Energy Analysis*, 1979

RIGHT: Janice Nease,
Anthropometrics Space Analysis, 1979

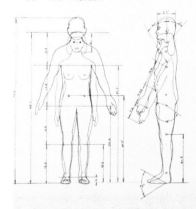

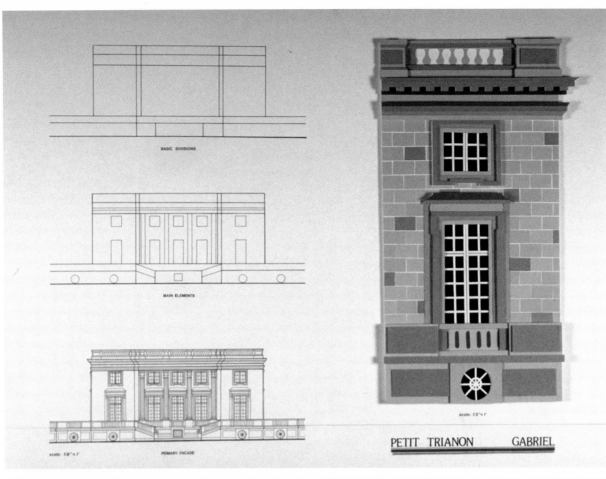

BASIC DIVISIONS

MAIN ELEMENTS

PRIMARY FACADE

scale: 1/8" = 1'

scale: 1/2" = 1'

PETIT TRIANON   GABRIEL

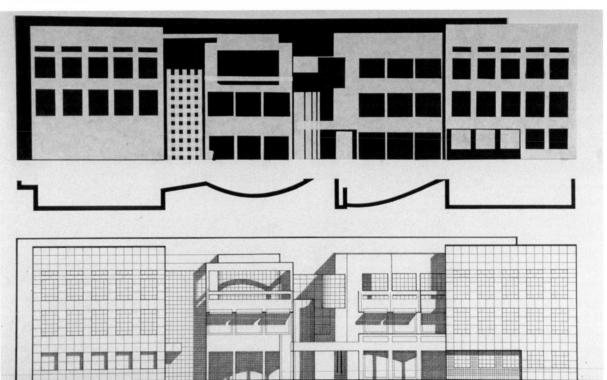

TOP: Chris Hatfield, 1985

BOTTOM: Brian Paul Kish, 1985

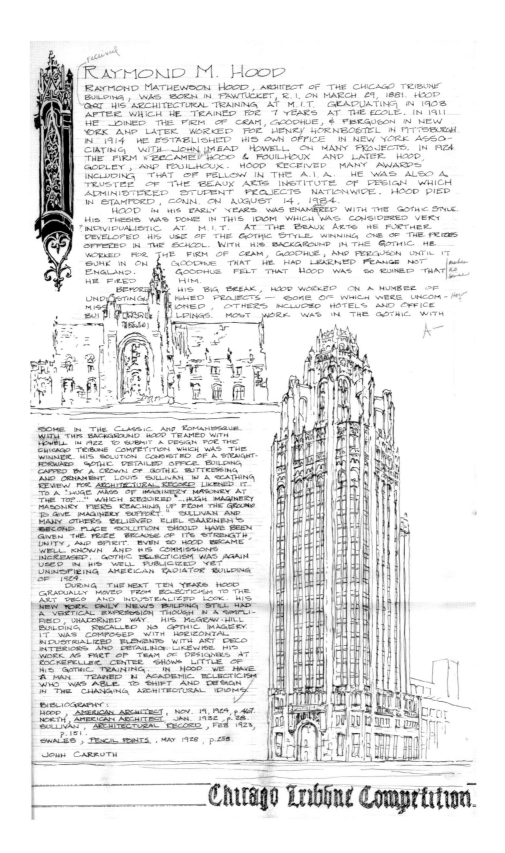

HISTORY AND DESIGN

Theory as a topic independent from architectural history rises as a significant academic concern over the last three decades. Prior to 1980 the teaching of history and design were intertwined. The creation of precedent studies in both history classes and studios was employed as a means of instruction. More recently, the study of theory involves intellectual research separate from the examination of built work.

Depicted here are precendent studies created for studios and a typical homework assignment in Frank Beckum's History of Modern Architecture course.

DEDICATION OF THE NEW WING

Beginning in 1972, students held frequent sit-ins to protest insufficient studio space for the growing number of architecture students. One of William L. "Bill" Fash's first projects as dean was the supervision of the construction of the new architecture building, now known as West Architecture, designed by Jerome Cooper. Marking the seventy-fifth anniversary of the Architecture Program at Georgia Tech, the much-anticipated dedication of the new wing was held during the fall of 1980. The Georgia Tech student chapter of the American Institute of Architects hosted a variety of activities to commemorate the grand opening of the new wing, themed "Transitions." The students held guided tours and promoted architectural interests on campus. In addition, this event inspired renovations and, essentially, a rebirth, of the original Architecture building, which had opened in 1952. Student, faculty, and alumni work was prominently displayed throughout both buildings. Notable guests and alumni, such as John C. Portman, B ARCH 1950, attended the gala to address the student body on architectural education and architecture as a business.

Jerome M. Cooper, FAIA, is a founding partner in the architectural firm of Cooper Carry and Associates. He received his Bachelor of Science in Architecture in 1952, then completed the Bachelor of Architecture in 1955. In 1956, he was a Fulbright Fellow at the University of Rome. Cooper was the principal designer for the West Architecture Building. The design process began in 1976 under contract with the firm of Cooper Carry and Associates. With its completion in 1980, all of the College of Architecture's programs were again in one location (with the exception of city planning). The building featured 57,000 square feet of badly needed studio space, four new seminar and classrooms, a computer laboratory, faculty, and administrative offices, and an expanded Architecture Library. In addition, laboratory space was created to support the rapidly growing research programs of the College.

Raymond E. Clark, *A Building for High School/Commercial*
Ink, Watercolor, Airbrush on Board, 30 x 40 inches
Board 1 of 4, Second Year Graduate Studio, 1978

Kent Knight, *McDonald's*
ASC/AIA Student Design Competition
Sponsored by McDonald's, First Place
Pen and Ink, 30 x 30 inches
Studio Critic Bob Segrest, 1979
Courtesy of Kent Knight

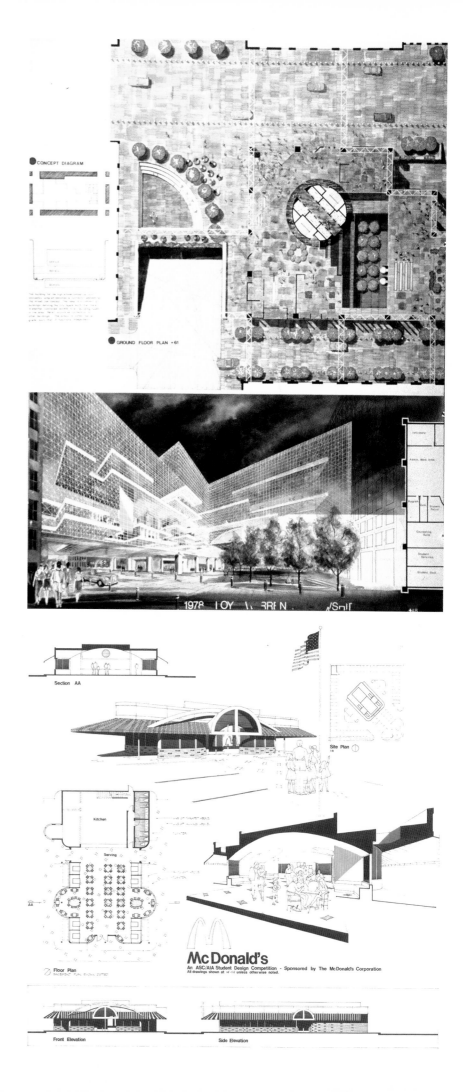

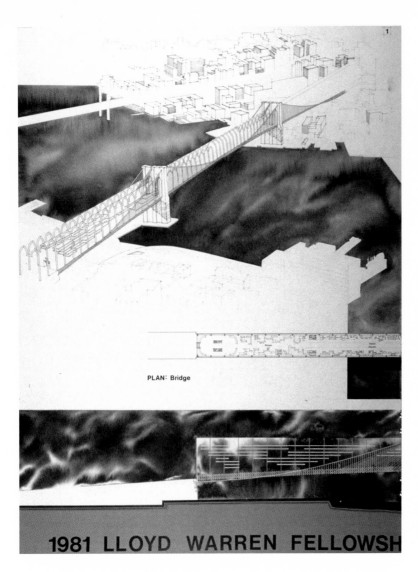

Ross S. Ransom, *A Brooklyn Bridge*, Lloyd Warren Fellowship - 68th Annual Paris Prize in Architecture, Ink, Airbrush, Photos on Board, 30 x 40 inches, Board 1 of 4 Second Year Graduate Studio, 1981

Linda J. D'Orazio, *A Brooklyn Bridge*, Lloyd Warren Fellowship - 68th Annual Paris Prize in Architecture, Ink, Airbrush, Photos on Board, 30 x 40 inches, Board 1 of 4 Second Year Graduate Studio, 1981

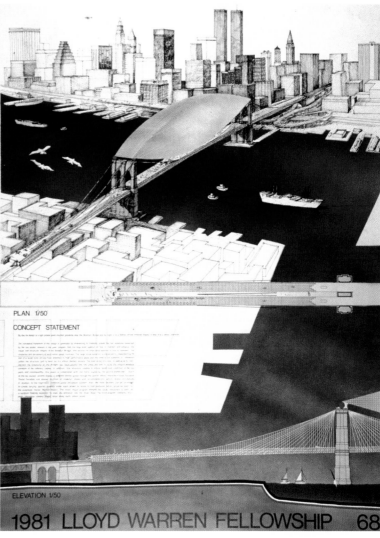

Gary E. Greene, *A Brooklyn Bridge*, Lloyd Warren Fellowship - 68th Annual Paris Prize
in Architecture, Ink, Airbrush, Photos on Board, 30 x 40 inches, Board 1 of 4
Second Year Graduate Studio, 1981

Brian H. Terrell, *A Brooklyn Bridge*, Lloyd Warren Fellowship - 68th Annual Paris Prize
in Architecture, Ink, Airbrush, Photos on Board, 30 x 40 inches, Board 1 of 4
Second Year Graduate Studio, 1981

AIAS AND SHUTZE ALUMNI AWARD

Beginning in the first years of the Architecture Program, students created clubs for social and professional activities. The first club of any type at Georgia Tech was the Artists Club initiated in 1910. More recently, the student chapter of the American Institute of Architects (AIAS) proved to have some years of extremely strong leadership that shaped activities within the College of Architecture. Such was the case in the early 1980s when Ken Gwinner, AIA, BS ARCH 1979, M ARCH 1983, served as the chapter president. To raise funds for their activities, the students ran a print shop from a space on the second floor bridge between the two buildings. In 1981, the AIAS initiated the Philip Trammell Shutze Distinguished Alumni Award and requested a medallion design from Professor Emeritus Julian Harris, BS ARCH 1928, a nationally recognized sculptor. The first recipient was Philip Shutze, BS ARCH 1912, who received the award in a ceremony presided over by the director Alan Balfour, who would later return as the dean of the College. In 1982, twelve members of the AIAS made a road trip to Lincoln, Nebraska, to place their bid for the National AIAS convention. Their memorable trip was successful, and the 1983 Forum held at Georgia Tech drew the largest participation of any national student meeting up to that time. The AIAS chapter continues to provide students an opportunity to be involved in a profession-centered organization.

KATHY BRACKNEY AND ARCHITECTURE LIBRARY

Over the years, the Georgia Tech Architecture Library has been an integral component of the College of Architecture. It is still the only branch library on campus. The first library was the design centerpiece of P. M. Heffernan's East Architecture Building, located in the space now occupied by the Imagine Lab. In 1980, the library moved to its current location in the West Architecture Building. For twenty-five years, from 1982 to 2007, Kathy Brackney served as head of the Architecture Library. This was a period of dramatic change, as the Georgia Tech Libraries entered the digital age. The Architecture Library's book collection also grew substantially, with support from an endowment fund established by Preston S. Stevens, Jr., B ARCH 1952, M ARCH 1953, in 1986 to honor the ninetieth birthday of his father, Preston S. Stevens, Sr., class of 1919. The Architecture Library collection was renamed the Preston S. Stevens, Sr. Architectural Collection.

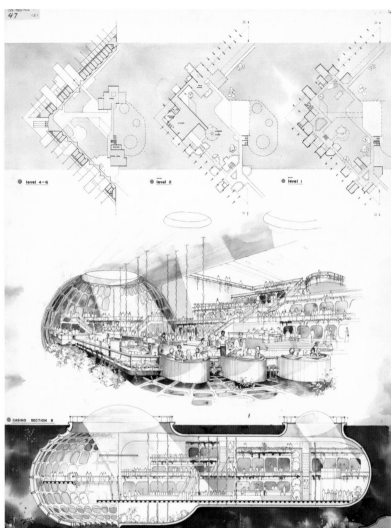

Mark D. Tilden, *Casino Hotel*, Lloyd Warren Fellowship - 66th Annual Paris Prize in Architecture, Honorable Mention, Ink, Watercolor, 30 x 40 inches, Board 3 of 5, Second Year Graduate Studio, 1979, Courtesy of Van Alen Institute's Design Competitions Archive

Rebecca L. Tyson, *Apple Computer Corporate Headquarters*
Ink, Airbrush on Board, 40 x 30 inches, Boards 1 and 2 of 3
Second Year Graduate Studio, 1984

HEJDUK CUBES

Architect John Hejduk drew inspiration for *House of the Suicide* and *House of the Mother of the Suicide* from Cezanne's painting, *The Funeral of Jan Palach* and David Shapiro's poem of the same name. In 1986, architecture students at Georgia Tech, led by studio critic James Williamson, collaborated with Hejduk on construction of the pieces. The process took nearly four years with twelve students examining the concept in a design process that included drawings, models, and full-scale mock-ups.

The resulting two art pieces occupied the central spaces of the first and second floors of the West Architecture Building. The inspiring presence of sculptural art could not withstand the extreme need for jury space. In 2002, Dean Thomas D. Galloway found a permanent home for the two works at the Whitney Museum of American Art in New York City.

Courtesy of Georgia Tech

When I entered the first meditation,
I escaped the gravity of the object,
I experienced the emptiness,
And I have been dead a long time.

When I had a voice you could call a voice,
My mother wept to me:
My son, my beloved son,
I never thought this possible,

I'll follow you on foot.
Halfway in mud and slush the microphones picked up.
It was raining on the houses;
It was snowing on the police-cars.

The astronauts were weeping,
Growing neither up nor out.
And my own mother was brave enough she looked
And it was alright I was dead.

"The Funeral of Jan Palach"
—by David Shapiro

COMPUTERS COME TO CAMPUS

In November 1984, Dean William L. "Bill" Fash invited Anatoliusz "Tolek" Lesniewski to teach a course on computer-aided design and thus began the academic use of computers in the Architecture Program. The college was given four IBM PC computers with dual floppy disks for this purpose. This first computer cluster was located in Room 358, which also served as Lesniewski's "office." For this first lab, Lesniewski and his assistants built the furniture and purchased parts to build more computers. In the summer of 1985 Fash asked him to continue as a full-time research engineer in the College of Architecture. He taught programming for architects and one AutoCAD class per quarter until 1990, when another instructor took over AutoCAD giving Lesniewski the opportunity to begin teaching 3-D modeling with DOS-based 3-D STUDIO program.

Lyle Green, *Rock-n-Roll Cemetery*, Collage Model, Second Year Graduate Studio, Studio Critic Merrill Elam, 1988

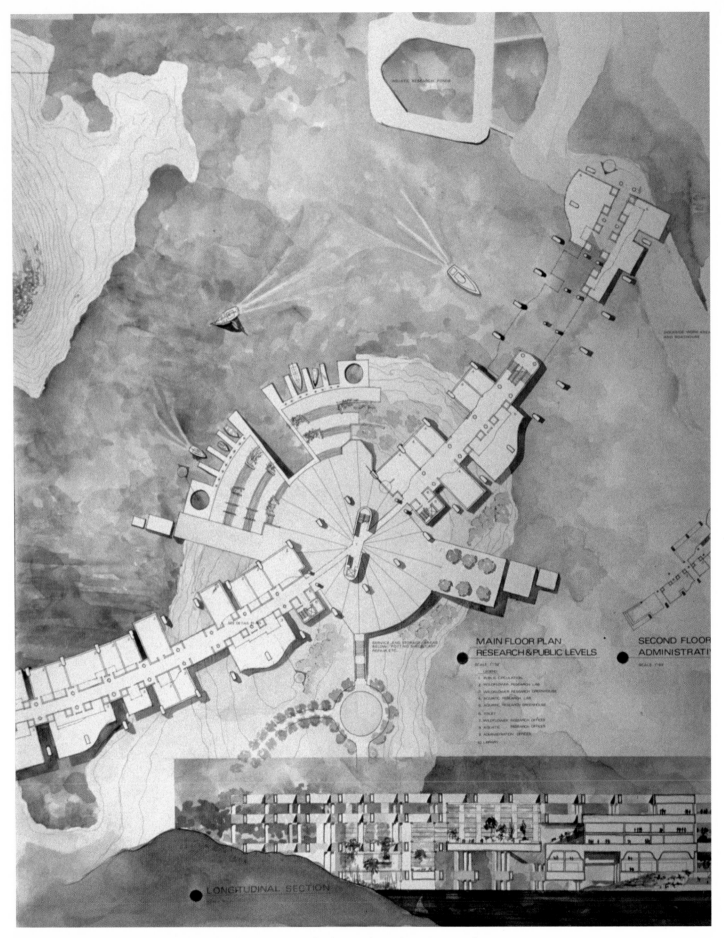

Author Unidentified, *National Center for Botanical Study*, Lloyd Warren Fellowship - 73rd Annual Paris Prize in Architecture
Ink, Watercolor, 30 x 40 inches, Board 2 of 4, Second Year Graduate Studio, 1986

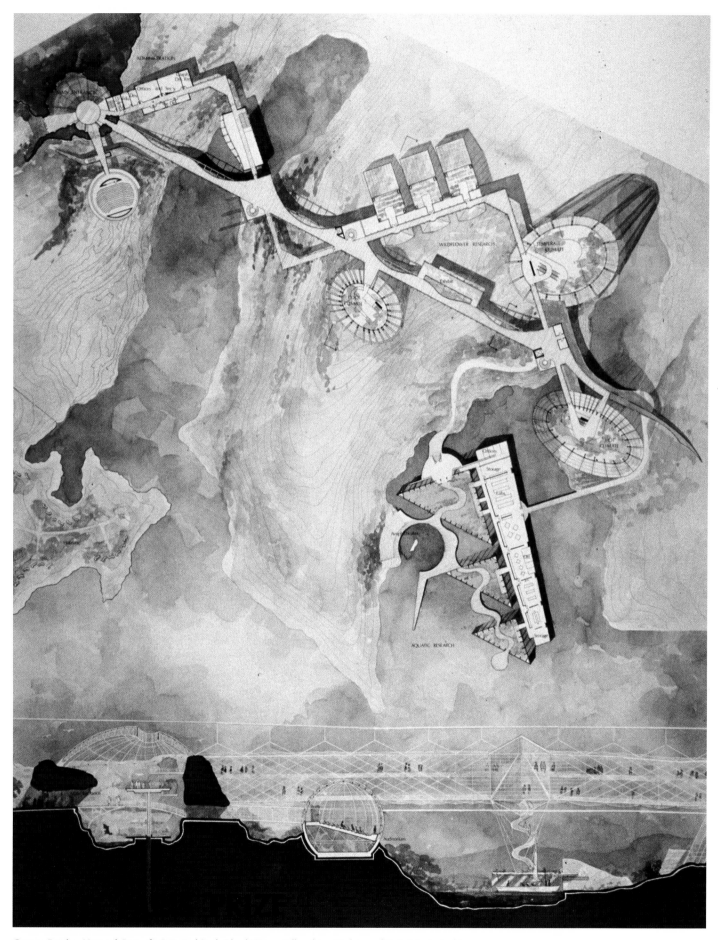

Carmen Ponder, *National Center for Botanical Study*, Lloyd Warren Fellowship - 73rd Annual Paris Prize in Architecture
Ink, Watercolor, 30 x 40 inches, Board 2 of 4, Second Year Graduate Studio, 1986

OPPOSITE: Dale McClain, *Development of the New Orleans Waterfront*
Lloyd Warren Fellowship - 69th Paris Prize in Architecture, First Prize, 1982

ABOVE: Sam van Nostrand, *Buckhead Branch Library*
Terminal Project, Senior Design
Studio Critic George Johnston, 1988

LEFT: Denise Dumais, *Biblioteque Municipal des Gobelins, Paris*
Chipboard, Colored Paper Model, Fourth Year Design, Paris Program
Studio Critic Richard Dagenhart, 1986

BELOW: Samuel Boyd, William Ruark, James Curry, Edwin Fulton, Ian Cha
Marcus Judge, David Khalili, John Pollard, Susan Smith, *Piazza di Este*
Third International Exhibition of Architecture, Venice Biennale
Museumboard, Chipboard Model, Senior Design
Studio Critic George Johnston, 1984

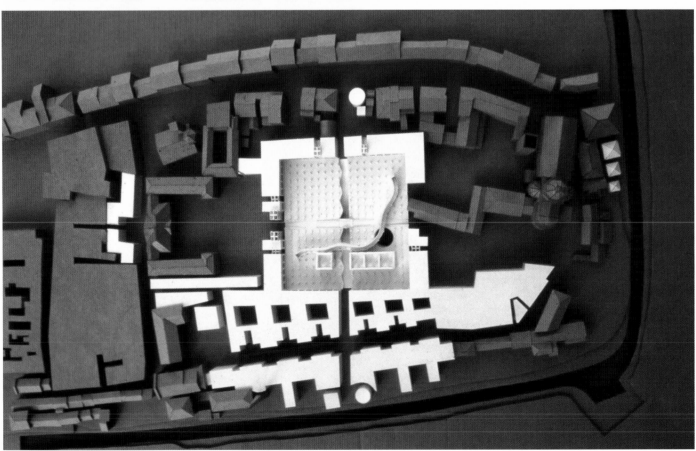

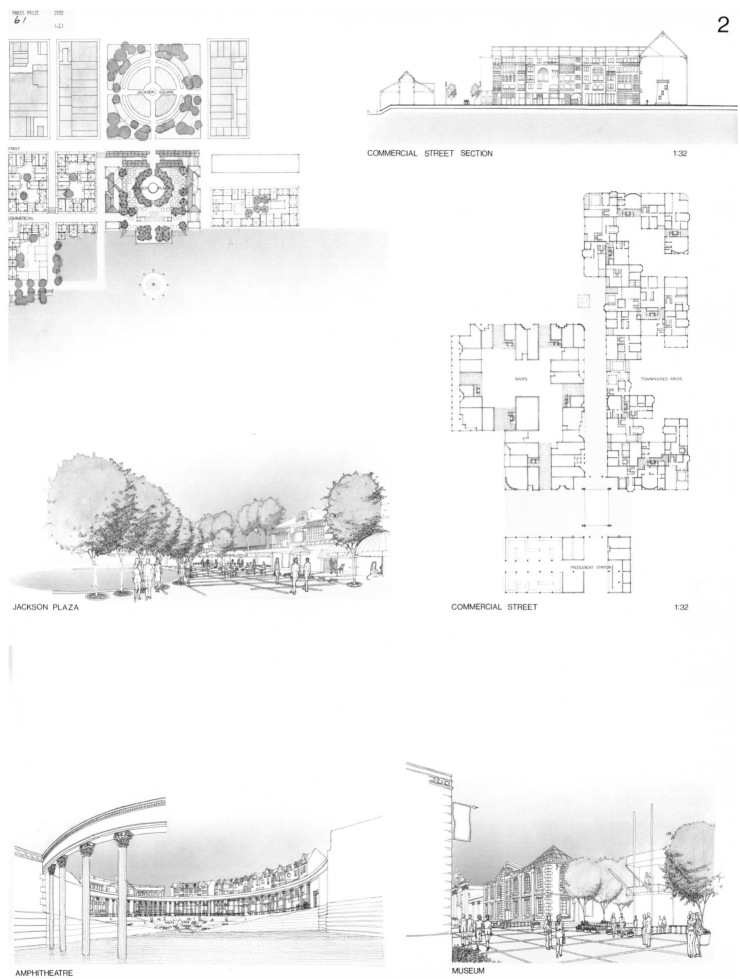

COMMERCIAL STREET SECTION   1:32

SHOPS

TOWNHOUSES ABOVE

PADDLEBOAT STATION

JACKSON PLAZA

COMMERCIAL STREET   1:32

AMPHITHEATRE

MUSEUM

ARCHITECTURE : NEW ORLEANS RIVERFRONT DEVELOPMENT

BASTILLE

Harris Dimitropoulos won the 1989 international competition to commemorate the French Revolution with his entry titled *Bastilles*. The concept of the site sculpture proposed an object lesson in the universality of the principles of the French Revolution and was built at the Parc de la Villette in Paris. The architectural sculpture included bricks imprinted with the words "Liberté, Égalité, Fraternité," and arranged in an equilateral triangle of twenty-eight cylinders. The visitors were invited to demolish the project and appropriate the bricks as souvenirs in a symbolic reenactment of the actual storming of the Bastille. Over the course of the exhibit, visitors also had the freedom to create new arrangements with the bricks.

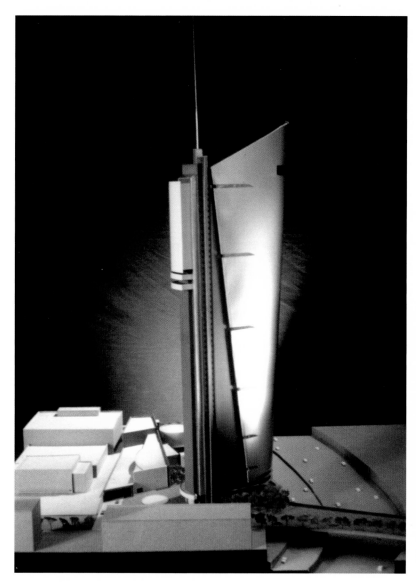

Robert Rule, *Corporate Headquarters for Delta, Midtown*
Chipboard, Colored Paper at 1/32" scale
Second Year Graduate Studio,
Tall Building Studio Critic Dale Durfee, 1990
Courtesy of Rob Rule

Author Unidentified
Watercolor Rendering, 40 x 30 inches
Second Year Graduate Studio
Tall Building Studio Critic Dale Durfee, 1990

Thomas D. Galloway, PHD, AICP

In 1992, Dean William L. "Bill" Fash stepped down as dean due to health reasons. An international search resulted in the hire of Thomas D. Galloway (1939-2007) who came to the College of Architecture at Georgia Tech from the College of Design at Iowa State University, where he served as dean and professor from 1985 to 1992. He also held faculty and administrative appointments at the University of Rhode Island and the University of Kansas. He completed his undergraduate degree in sociology at Westmont College in Santa Barbara, California, in 1962 and completed his master's and PhD degrees in urban planning at the University of Washington in 1969 and 1972, respectively. In the decade and a half of his leadership, Galloway made lasting changes as dean. In addition to strengthening the academic and research areas of the College, he created the Development Council to gain advice and counsel from recognized leaders among the alumni of the College. Of special significance to this exhibit, he secured the P. M. Heffernan House for the College and designated a part of it as the archive for student work that for decades had languished untended in a storage room in the East Architecture Building.

ART AND ARCHITECTURE IN GREECE AND ITALY

In 1993, Elizabeth "Betty" Meredith Dowling initiated the first College of Architecture summer foreign program with a five-week study of Italian art and architecture spanning from the ancient world through the Baroque seventeenth century. Based originally in Rome, but expanded to include Greece and Northern Italy, the instructional concept used the on-site study of architecture, museums, and urban spaces as the sole classroom. Students will forever recall living in the oldest hotel in Rome, the Albergo Sole, built on the foundations of the Theater of Pompey where Julius Caesar was assassinated. Beginning in 1994, Professor Douglas C. Allen joined the program assuming responsibility for the ancient Roman world. Using the material record of Rome, Ostia, Pompeii, Herculaneum, and Paestum, students from all disciplines at Georgia Tech learned of the profound debt Western civilization owes to the ancient Mediterranean world. This learning experience was expanded in 2006 when Professor Athanassios "Thanos" Economou joined the program and added depth to this study by clarifying the sources of Roman civilization in the ancient Greek world. Over the years, the program developed with Dowling taking charge of the Renaissance periods and moving with the group northward to Florence, Siena, Venice, and Vicenza with periodic excursions to Assisi, Caprarola, Mantua, and Verona. Professor Franca Trubiano will add new energy to the program beginning in 2009, as she becomes the lead professor of the Renaissance era. Through the years, almost four hundred students from all majors at Georgia Tech have learned to appreciate urban life, Mediterranean civilization, and the vast beauty of the art and architecture of Greece and Italy.

MODERN ARCHITECTURE AND THE MODERN CITY

Professor Richard Dagenhart founded the European summer abroad program Modern Architecture and the Modern City in 1991 with a small seed grant from the Georgia Tech Foundation. The original objective for the program, which has been maintained for the past eighteen years, was to provide additional breadth and depth of knowledge in modern and contemporary architecture and urban design for Georgia Tech graduate students. The first year included extended visits to Berlin, Paris, Florence, and Rome, with Georgia Tech faculty members Richard Dagenhart, Randall Roark, and Libero Andreotti and fifteen graduate students. With the increasing importance of Dutch architecture in the 1990s, the program began to include extended visits to the Netherlands, as well as Berlin and Paris. Soon after, a brief visit to another city was added to the program, beginning with Barcelona, which is a perennial favorite, along with Copenhagen, Stockholm, Helsinki, and Vienna. The faculty involved in the program have included Richard Dagenhart (Berlin, Paris, the Netherlands, Barcelona, and Scandinavia), Michael Gamble (Berlin and Scandinavia), David Green (Paris), Chris Jarrett (Paris), Mark Cottle (Barcelona), Frances Hsu (Vienna), Elliot Pavlos (Paris and Amsterdam), Libero Andreotti (Florence and Rome), and Annette Fiero (Paris and Amsterdam). More than two hundred graduate students have participated in the program, visiting the most important monuments of modern architecture and urban design, exploring the leading contemporary projects built during the past twenty years, attending lectures and exhibitions, preparing research projects, essays, and journals, and enjoying life in some of the great and humane cities of the world.

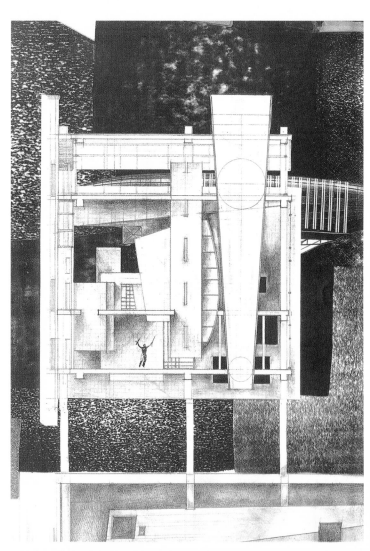

LEFT: Jonathan LaCrosse, *Artist's Studio and Residence*
Velux Prize, First Place, Graphite on Watercolor paper
40 x 30 inches, Board 1 of 5, Junior Design, 1997

BELOW: T. Jade Binnerts, *East Lake Meadows Public Housing*
Cardboard, Chipboard Model, Second Year Graduate Studio
Studio Critic Richard Dagenhart, 1992

BOTTOM: Robert Rule, *Morphogenesis*, SGF Prize, First Place
Chipboard, Museumboard Model, 32 x 60 inches
Second Year Graduate Studio
Studio Critic Richard Dagenhart, 1990

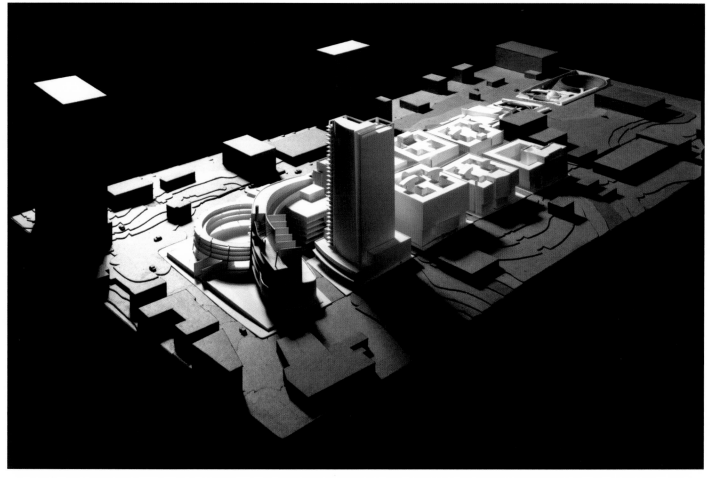

1996 SUMMER OLYMPICS

Georgia Tech's role in research for the 1996 Summer Olympics began long before Atlanta was awarded the bid to host the games. President John Crecine enlisted Georgia Tech to help create three-dimensional computer models/renderings to aid in marketing the city for the Olympics. Collaborating with Georgia State University and local private companies, Anatoliusz "Tolek" Lesniewski and his team of researchers, including John Cleveland as computer coordinator, pioneered a high-technology multimedia interactive program for the 1990 final proposal to the International Olympic Committee in Tokyo. Their project received the Computerworld Smithsonian Award in 1992 and a New Media Invision Award for Olympic Presentations in 1994. At this time, Georgia Tech's College of Architecture was leading the Institute in multimedia technology.

The firm of Stanley, Love-Stanley, P.C., teamed up with Smallwood, Reynolds, Stewart, Stewart & Associates to design and construct the Olympic Aquatic Center at Georgia Tech (1995-1996), which has become the campus's most significant memorial to the Olympic Games.

COMMON FIRST YEAR

Georgia Tech's conversion of the academic calendar in 1999 from a quarter to a semester system provided the impetus for instituting major academic changes in the College of Architecture. The most significant of these concerned the implementation of a multidisciplinary, ten-credit hour, studio- and lecture-based curriculum required of all freshmen majoring in the College. Termed CFY for the Common First Year, the curriculum combines two studio courses and one lecture course to address issues of design at many scales—products, buildings, systems, and environments. Sabir Khan, associate professor and associate dean, conceived of this iteration of the CFY. In describing this innovative course, Khan writes, "The animating desire of the curriculum is to sponsor and support a curiosity about the world (and everything in it) and to provide the tools with which to engage this world in all its potential complexity and immediacy. Given both our pedagogical emphasis on collective learning and the logistics of the teaching space (up to sixteen sections each semester within a 'hot-desk' format with four students to a desk), the exercises unfold in a wide range of discursive situations: individual, small-group, and collective desk-crits, pin-ups, chalkboard talks, and online commentary." Each semester the 200-plus students and sixteen instructors interact in the design teaching and learning process using COOL, a collaborative online Web site. The recipient of a Progressive Architecture Research Award, COOL has evolved from a prototype Khan and Professor Craig Zimring developed ten years ago.

ABOVE LEFT: Bill Stanley and Ivenue Love-Stanley at the Olympic Aquatic Center at Georgia Tech
ABOVE RIGHT: Sabir Khan, 1996

RIGHT: Merica May Jensen, *Riff,* Exercise 3 Design Explorations
Digital Rendering, 18 x 24 inches, Common First Year
Studio Critic Carina Antunez, 2008

BELOW: Jonathan Baker, Charcoal Drawing, Chipboard Model
Common First Year, Studio Critic Wilfredo Rodriguez, 2002

BOTTOM: Authors Unidentified, *Competition Mecanoo, Riva del Garda, Italy*
Paris Prize, Digital Rendering, Photomontage, 30 x 40 inches, Fourth Year
Design, Studio Critics Mark Cottle, Libero Andreotti, Xavier Wrona, 2006

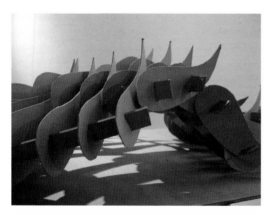

In 2002 William H. "Bill" Harrison, B ARCH 1971, and Gregory L. Palmer, principals in Harrison Design Associates, commenced a gift leading to a $500,000 endowment in honor of Elizabeth Dowling and her area of specialization in traditional and classical architecture that is a shared interest of the firm. This significant gift marked only the second major endowment in the program's history. The firm of Harrison Design Associates is one of the largest practices in traditional design in the country with four offices in Georgia and California. A portion of the endowment is used each year to bring in a variety of architects as visiting scholars to share their expertise with students through studio- and classroom-based instruction. From 2003 to 2007, the endowment sponsored five architects who offered courses in areas related to classical design. Eugene L. Surber, BS ARCH 1961, taught a studio in the documentary measurement and compatible design. Anne Fairfax, principal with Farifax and Sammons in New York, Charleston, and Palm Beach, taught a studio concerned with the study of local vocabulary in order to insert a building in a historic neighborhood. Gregory Saldana, president of Saldana Design & Preservation Inc., taught a course on measured drawings and archival research. Richard Sammons, principal of Fairfax and Sammons, taught an elective course on proportion that is the subject of an upcoming book on his research and application of proportion in design. Christine Franck, principal of Christine G.H. Franck, Inc., co-taught an elective course with Betty Dowling on ornament and historically inspired design. With the initiation of a master of science degree with an emphasis in classical design in 2007, the Harrison Visiting Scholar assumed the role of studio instructor during the spring term for the new program. Richard John, assistant professor at the University of Miami, provided the first studio and in spring 2009, Michael Mesko, principal with MSM Design and Planning in New York, offered the second one in classical design.

LEFT: Paul Knight, *The American House Today: Designing with Style, Two-Story Residence for Macon, Georgia*
Ink, Watercolor on Arches Paper, 40 x 30 inches, Analytique, Elective course, Christine Franck, Harrison Design Associates Visiting Scholar, 2007

RIGHT: David Pearson, *Wall Street Ferry Terminal*, Pen and Ink, Watercolor, 40 x 30 inches, Analytique, First Year Studio, MS/Classical Design, 2007

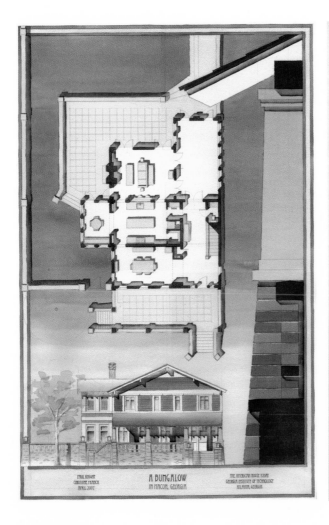

LEFT AND RIGHT: Bill Davis, *Fifth Street Bridge*, SGF Prize, First Place, Digital Rendering Photomontage, 30 x 40 inches, Boards 2 and 3 of 6, Second Year Graduate Studio, 2000

Ellen Dunham-Jones

After several years of turnover in leadership, Ellen Dunham-Jones was hired and has served as the director of the Architecture Program since 2001. She received undergraduate and graduate degrees in architecture from Princeton University and taught at University of Virginia and the Massachusetts Institute of Technology. The problematic suburban existence of Atlanta proved to be an attractive incentive for her to lead the program, as her scholarly interests relate to developing creative and critical improvements to the everyday landscape. She has developed new linkages with the professional community through her position on the Board of Directors of the Congress for the New Urbanism. An advocate for alternatives to sprawl, she is co-author with June Williamson of *Retrofitting Suburbia: Urban Design Solutions for Redesigning Suburbs* (John Wiley & Sons, 2008); and she has published more than fifty articles in leading design journals and books. In the 2006-2007 academic year, she was the Ax:son Johnson Institute guest professor at Lund University in Lund, Sweden.

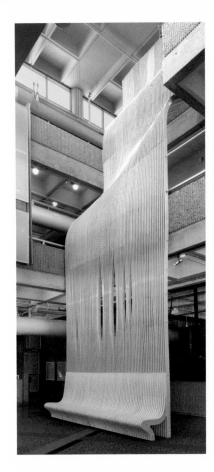

VENTULETT DISTINGUISHED CHAIR

Thomas W. Ventulett, III, FAIA, B ARCH 1958, principal in the Atlanta architectural firm of Thompson, Ventulett, Stainback, and Associates (TVS), maintained a strong relationship with Georgia Tech's College of Architecture by participating in accreditation evaluations, lecturing on his work, and hiring and training graduates. The first endowed architecture chair in Georgia, the Thomas W. Ventulett, III Distinguished Chair in Architectural Design at Georgia Tech, was an endeavor funded by his firm, family, and friends.

With a funded endowed architectural chair, superlative students and faculty are attracted to the program and the College receives international recognition for the research conducted through the position. Teachers and scholars are also drawn towards the vitality of this pioneering invention in architectural education, augmenting the curriculum and collaboration between colleges within the Institute.

In 2004, Monica Ponce de Leon was selected to receive the first Ventulett Distinguished Chair. Ponce de Leon was an Associate Professor teaching design studios and courses in visual studies/ecological fabrication in the Harvard Graduate School of Design and a principal in one of the most innovative design firms in the United States. She co-founded the firm Office dA with Nader Tehrani, and became known for her contributions to green, sustainable design and urban planning. Ponce de Leon is currently dean at the University of Michigan Taubman College of Architecture + Urban Planning.

Nader Tehrani, also a principal in the firm of Office dA, was awarded the second position of the Ventulett Distinguished Chair in 2005. Focusing on the research of materials, patterning, methods of aggregations, geometry, and the advancement of digital fabrication, Tehrani's studios primarily researched new methods of fabrication through digital design. The Nader installation, an aggregate form relating to cellular division and reformation, exemplifies the type of installation achieved by the students under his direction. The polycarbonate form created from 1,500 customized pieces made by a numerically controlled router remains suspended on the façade of the West Architecture building.

ABOVE LEFT: *Rapunzel,* three-story bench, Asa Martin, Paul Erhet, Richard Aeck, Fabrication Workshop, Studio Critic Monica Ponce de Leon, 2005

ABOVE RIGHT AND OPPOSITE: Installation on south facade of West Architecture Building, Brandon Clifford, Lorraine Ong, Vishwadeep Deo, Mohamed Mohson, Richard Aeck, Daniel Baron, Brandi Flannagan, Vinay Shiposkar, Jonathan Baker, Fabrication Workshop, Studio Critic Nader Tehrani, Co-Instructor Tristan Al-Haddad, 2006

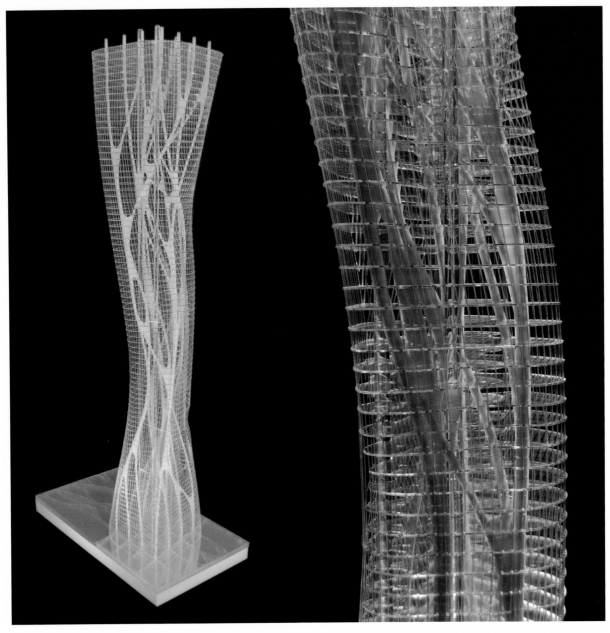

Models by Matthew Erwin and Adam Sauer, Textile Tectonics Studio, Ventulett Competition, First Place
Second Year Graduate Studio, Studio Critic Lars Spuybroek, Co-Instructor Daniel Baerlecken, 2008

In 2006, Lars Spuybroek was named the third Thomas W. Ventulett III Distinguished Chair in Architectural Design. Spuybroek is the principal of NOX architecture studio in Rotterdam, Holland. Since the early nineties he has been researching the relationship between art, architecture and computing not only by building but also by writing, speaking, and teaching. He received international recognition after building the Water Pavilion (HtwoOexpo) in 1997, the first building in the world fully incorporating new media. In 2004, NOX finished the D-Tower, the Son-O-house and a cluster of cultural buildings in Lille, France (Maison Folies). In the same year Thames & Hudson published his monograph, *NOX: Machining Architecture.*

Solar Decathlon House on the National Mall Washington, D.C., Fall 2007
Courtesy of Georgia Tech

SOLAR DECATHLON 2007

In January 2006, faculty members Ruchi Choudhary, Russell Gentry, Chris Jarrett, and Franca Trubiano were awarded $100,000 and invited to participate in the 2007 Solar Decathlon Competition sponsored by the U.S. Department of Energy and the National Renewable Energy Laboratory. The international competition between twenty universities involved the design, construction, and testing of a zero-energy single-family home entirely powered by solar technologies. Over the course of two years, students and faculty from the Architecture, Industrial Design, and Building Construction programs worked in an interdisciplinary fashion with the Colleges of Engineering, Sciences, and Management. Innovative pedagogical collaborations included engineering workshops, vertically oriented design studios, and design-build activities. Important relationships were forged with partners from the building construction industry and solar technology suppliers. Many of the project's details highlighted the fabrication potential of the College's Advanced Wood Products Lab and the representational potential of the Imagine Lab. The house was designed through a collaborative process and its construction and engineering involved student leaders Jason Brown, Jason Mabry, Joe Jamgochian, Matt Erwin, Vishwadeep Deo, Alstan Jakubiec, Amelia Mendez, and Arseni Zaitsev. Professors Choudhary, Gentry, and Trubiano supervised the construction of this 800sf solar-powered house during the summer 2007. The house was transported to the National Mall in Washington, D.C., in October 2007 where it received the BP Innovation Award. Upon its return, the house remained on campus for one year and hosted thousands of visitors ranging from school children to the Chancellor of the Board of Regents. In December 2008, Green Habitats Foundation, the stewardship sponsor of the house, oversaw its relocation on the grounds of the Tellus Northwest Georgia Science Museum in Cartersville.

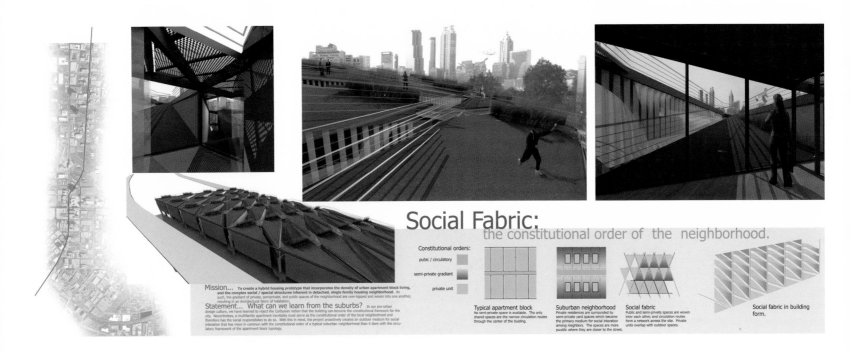

PORTMAN PRIZE

Founded in 2000, the Portman Prize Competition, funded by the office of John C. Portman, Jr., BS 1950, and his son Jack Portman, B Arch 1971, is an important annual event of the College of Architecture that recognizes the best work from the Options I Graduate Design Studios. In addition to bringing in a distinguished and diverse jury and the monetary awards for the first, second, and third prize winners, the Portman Prize also provides additional resources to bring in a noted professional relevant to the prize program. This scholar gives lectures and individual student critiques during the semester, and serves as one of the judges. Experts on housing brought to the college as Portman Critics have benefitted the intellectual life of the program. Thus far, the Portman critics have been David Baker, FAIA, of DB+P Architects in San Francisco in 2006; Julie Eizenberg of Koning Eizenberg Architecture in Santa Monica in 2007; and Jonathan Segal, FAIA, in San Diego in 2008.

ABOVE: Jonathan Aprati, *Social Fabric*, Portman Prize, First Place, Board 1 of 3, 48 x 96 inches
First Year Graduate Studio, Studio Critic Stuart Romm, 2007

OPPOSITE: Jerry Page, Christopher Van Kley, *Living Graft*, Integrating Habitats International Student Design Competition
Second Place, Team Leader Fred Pearsall, 2008

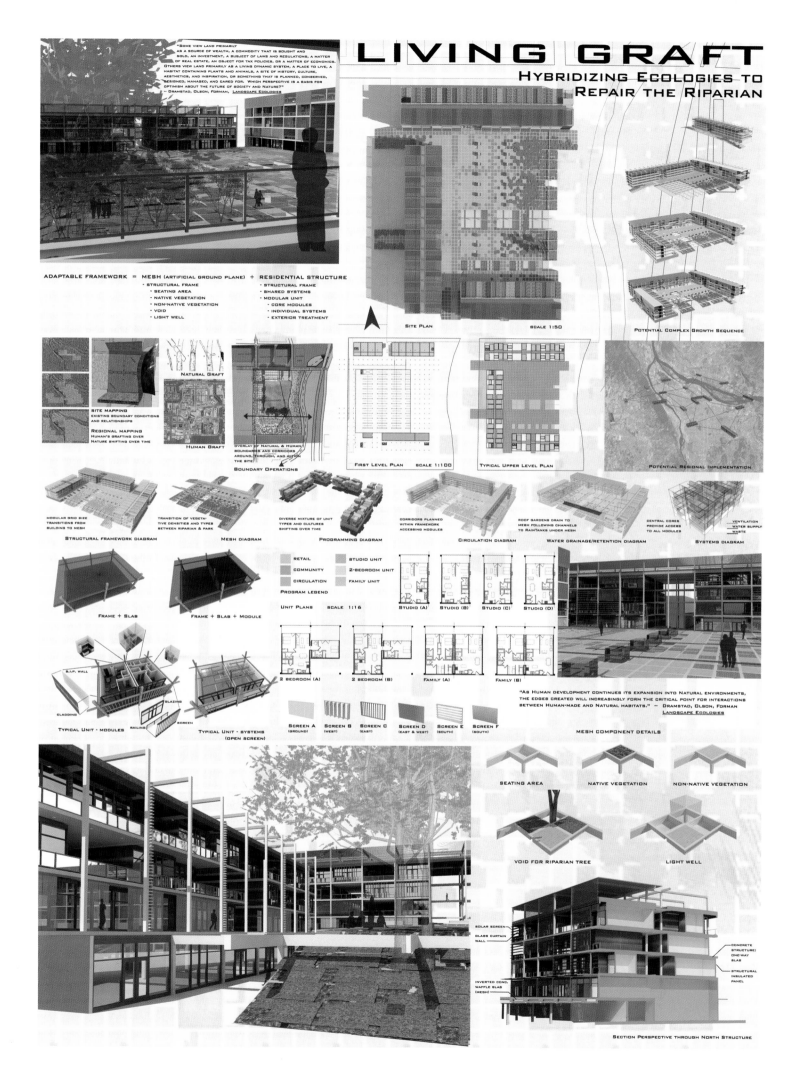

LIVING GRAFT
HYBRIDIZING ECOLOGIES TO REPAIR THE RIPARIAN

"SOME VIEW LAND PRIMARILY AS A SOURCE OF WEALTH, A COMMODITY THAT IS BOUGHT AND SOLD, AN INVESTMENT, A SUBJECT OF LAWS AND REGULATIONS, A MATTER OF REAL ESTATE, AN OBJECT FOR TAX POLICIES, OR A MATTER OF ECONOMICS. OTHERS VIEW LAND PRIMARILY AS A LIVING DYNAMIC SYSTEM, A PLACE TO LIVE, A HABITAT CONTAINING PLANTS AND ANIMALS, A SITE OF HISTORY, CULTURE, AESTHETICS, AND INSPIRATION, OR SOMETHING THAT IS PLANNED, CONSERVED, DESIGNED, MANAGED, AND CARED FOR. WHICH PERSPECTIVE IS A BASIS FOR OPTIMISM ABOUT THE FUTURE OF SOCIETY AND NATURE?" — DRAMSTAD, OLSON, FORMAN, LANDSCAPE ECOLOGIES

ADAPTABLE FRAMEWORK = MESH (ARTIFICIAL GROUND PLANE) + RESIDENTIAL STRUCTURE

- STRUCTURAL FRAME
  - SEATING AREA
  - NATIVE VEGETATION
  - NON-NATIVE VEGETATION
  - VOID
  - LIGHT WELL
- STRUCTURAL FRAME
  - SHARED SYSTEMS
  - MODULAR UNIT
    - CORE MODULES
    - INDIVIDUAL SYSTEMS
    - EXTERIOR TREATMENT

SITE PLAN   SCALE 1:50

POTENTIAL COMPLEX GROWTH SEQUENCE

NATURAL GRAFT

SITE MAPPING
EXISTING BOUNDARY CONDITIONS AND RELATIONSHIPS

REGIONAL MAPPING
HUMAN'S GRAFTING OVER NATURE SHIFTING OVER TIME

HUMAN GRAFT

OVERLAY OF NATURAL & HUMAN BOUNDARIES AND CORRIDORS AROUND, THROUGH, AND WITHIN THE SITE
BOUNDARY OPERATIONS

FIRST LEVEL PLAN   SCALE 1:100

TYPICAL UPPER LEVEL PLAN

POTENTIAL REGIONAL IMPLEMENTATION

MODULAR GRID SIZE TRANSITIONS FROM BUILDING TO MESH
STRUCTURAL FRAMEWORK DIAGRAM

TRANSITION OF VEGETATIVE DENSITIES AND TYPES BETWEEN RIPARIAN & PARK
MESH DIAGRAM

DIVERSE MIXTURE OF UNIT TYPES AND CULTURES SHIFTING OVER TIME
PROGRAMMING DIAGRAM

CORRIDORS PLANNED WITHIN FRAMEWORK ACCESSING MODULES
CIRCULATION DIAGRAM

ROOF GARDENS DRAIN TO MESH FOLLOWING CHANNELS TO RAINTANKS UNDER MESH
WATER DRAINAGE/RETENTION DIAGRAM

CENTRAL CORES PROVIDE ACCESS TO ALL MODULES
VENTILATION
WATER SUPPLY
WASTE
SYSTEMS DIAGRAM

PROGRAM LEGEND
- RETAIL
- COMMUNITY
- CIRCULATION
- STUDIO UNIT
- 2-BEDROOM UNIT
- FAMILY UNIT

UNIT PLANS   SCALE 1:16

STUDIO (A)   STUDIO (B)   STUDIO (C)   STUDIO (D)

FRAME + SLAB

FRAME + SLAB + MODULE

2 BEDROOM (A)   2 BEDROOM (B)   FAMILY (A)   FAMILY (B)

S.I.P. WALL
GLAZING
CLADDING
RAILING   SCREEN
TYPICAL UNIT - MODULES

TYPICAL UNIT - SYSTEMS
(OPEN SCREEN)

SCREEN A (GROUND)   SCREEN B (WEST)   SCREEN C (EAST)   SCREEN D (EAST & WEST)   SCREEN E (SOUTH)   SCREEN F (SOUTH)

"AS HUMAN DEVELOPMENT CONTINUES ITS EXPANSION INTO NATURAL ENVIRONMENTS, THE EDGES CREATED WILL INCREASINGLY FORM THE CRITICAL POINT FOR INTERACTIONS BETWEEN HUMAN-MADE AND NATURAL HABITATS." — DRAMSTAD, OLSON, FORMAN LANDSCAPE ECOLOGIES

MESH COMPONENT DETAILS

SEATING AREA   NATIVE VEGETATION   NON-NATIVE VEGETATION

VOID FOR RIPARIAN TREE   LIGHT WELL

SOLAR SCREEN
GLASS CURTAIN WALL
CONCRETE STRUCTURE; ONE-WAY SLAB
STRUCTURAL INSULATED PANEL
INVERTED CONC. WAFFLE SLAB (MESH)

SECTION PERSPECTIVE THROUGH NORTH STRUCTURE

LEFT: Jeff Williams, Chad Stacy, Scott d'Agostino, Shauna Achey
International Competition for Sustainable Design, Dubai, UAE, First Place
Team Leader Richard Dagenhart, 2008

OPPOSITE, TOP: Blake Burton, Tristan Hall, *Re-Life of a Terminal, Dallas, TX*
ACSA International Student Design Competition, First Place
Boards 2 and 3 of 4, Team Leader Harris Dimitropoulos, 2008

OPPOSITE, BOTTOM:
Presentation Team: Eric Polite, Donneice Wright, Reginald Tabor
Project Team: Joyce Gemarino, Sarah Turner, Jaren Abedania, Alphonso
Jordan, Will Gilbert, Sharod Alford
National Memorial and Interpretive Center of the Civil Rights Movement,
NOMAS Student Competition 2008, Second Place
Board 1 of 4, 24 x 36 inches
Studio Critics Herman Howard and Nekia Strong

Following an international search for the replacement of the late Dean Thomas D. Galloway, Alan Balfour became the third dean of the College of Architecture. His tenure as dean commenced in July 2008 and marks his return to Georgia Tech after two decades of administrative service in America and Britain. Following his work as the director of Architecture from 1978-1988, Balfour served as dean of architecture at Rice University in Texas and chairman of the Architecture Association in London from 1991 to 1995. During his tenure as dean of the School of Architecture at Rensselaer Polytechnic Institute from 1995 to 2008, he received the 2000 American Institute of Architects/Association of Collegiate Schools of Architecture (AIA/ACSA) Topaz Medallion for Excellence in Architectural Education, the highest recognition given to a North American architecture educator. This honor was due, in part, to his prolific work as an architectural writer. He created his World Cities series of books that explore architecture and urbanism of cities around the world, including *Shanghai* (2002), *New York* (2001), and *Berlin* (1995). For his books *Berlin* and *Berlin: The Politics of Order: 1737–1989* (1990), he received AIA International Book Awards. His recent book *Creating a Scottish Parliament* (2005) links the building's creation with the political structure of devolved Scotland. Balfour faces great challenges as the dean of a college composed of five academic units, seven research centers, 700-plus undergraduates and 500-plus graduate students, an immensely changed institution from the 1908 program created for twenty architecture students.

Balfour's vision for the College is one that anticipates changes in the building and design professions to create multidisciplinary professionals empowered by digital tools to manage the forces of development in a resource-constrained world and to create professionals who are able to project with confidence the impact of their plans and buildings fifty and hundred years into the future. Out of this could come not only a productive convergence between all the disciplines present in the College but new degrees across disciplines, leading eventually to new professions better able to define and address the challenges of an increasingly complex society. To prepare for this new direction, graduates of our programs must in the future have mastery of the tools and information created by digital technologies; must utilize these tools to predict the impact of their decisions at every scale on the world's increasingly scarce resources and community life; and must view their knowledge, creativity, and skill as being as essential and relevant to global as well as local practice. Amidst these imperatives, they must possess a feeling for and the ability to communicate the elegance of ideas in any field.

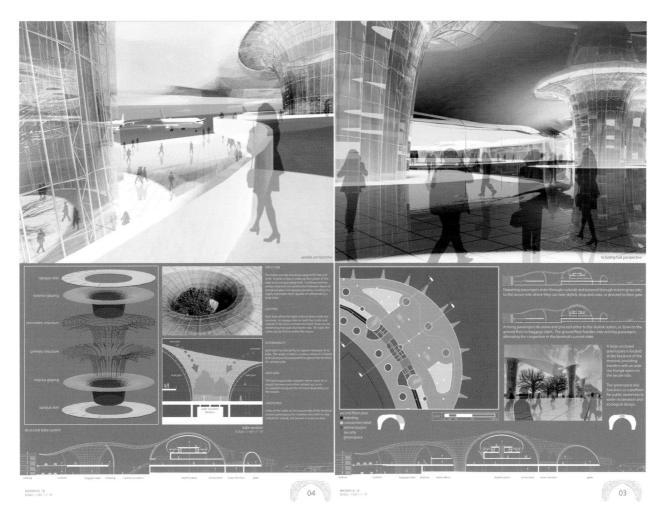

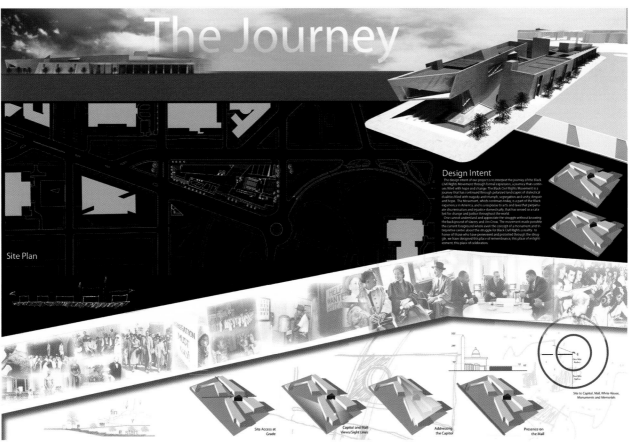

The Journey

Design Intent

The design intent of our project is to interpret the journey of the Black Civil Rights Movement through formal expression, a journey that continues filled with hope and change. The Black Civil Rights Movement is a journey that has continued through polarized landscapes of dialectical dualities filled with tragedy and triumph, segregation and unity, despair and hope. The Movement, which continues today, is a part of the Black experience in America, and is a response to acts and laws that perpetuate discrimination and injustice domestically, that has served as a catalyst for change and justice throughout the world.

One cannot understand and appreciate the struggle without knowing the background of slavery and Jim Crow. The movement made possible the current foreground where even the concept of a monument and interpretive center about the struggle for Black Civil Rights a reality. In honor of those who have persevered and protested through the struggle, we have designed this place of remembrance, this place of enlightenment, this place of celebration.

Site Plan

Site to Capitol, Mall, White House, Monuments and Memorials

Site Access at Grade

Capitol and Mall Views/Sight Lines

Addressing the Capitol

Presence on the Mall

Photographs from *The Next One Hundred Years* charette envisioning the architecture of the next century.

Periaktos, First Prize
Faculty Team Leader: Athanassios Economou
Student Team Members: Farzeen Tejani, Ali Lari, Youngju Lee, Ralph Raymond, Chris Martin, Christine Ruffo, Thang Pham, Ailien Vuong, Ana Lucia Gadala-Maria, Jordan Leary, John Nuttmann, Micah Hall, Andrew Nichols, Hector Caceres

Happy Bubble People, Second Prize
Faculty Team Leader: Mark Cottle
Student Team Members: Anand Amin, Andrew Hrycaj, Carolyn Knabel, Hsiang-Ming Wen, Katherine Solsten, Kirsten Wynkoop, Laura Lamar, Logan Tuura, Mihir Patel, Tyler Orlansky

Second Prize (tie)
Faculty Team Leader: Gernot Riether
Student Team Members: Alysha Buck, Emily Connor, Christina Deriso, Guo Jing, Kim Gyeong, Amyn Mukadam-Soldier, Chang Sup Lee, Inbeom Lee, Eric Morris, WenWen Zhao

Cybercorporeal, Third Prize
Faculty Team Leader: Harris Dimitropoulos
Sophia Bromfield, Colleen Creighton, Dane Hawthorne, Sal Lalani, Ken Mai, Christy Seerly, Taylor Smith, Pete Zhuangchen, Tim Wheelcock

Fabbrica Illuminato, Special Honorable Mention
Faculty Team Leader: Franca Trubiano
Keilah Everett, Kenneth Thompson, Joseph Vizuragga, Will Gilbert, Jiwon Huh, Erin Sherman, Eric Hawkins, John Brandes, Jessica Betel, Howard Wang, Jennifer Lewis, Leeland McPhail

Tenured and Tenure-Track Architecture Faculty, 2009

FIRST ROW: Ellen Dunham-Jones, George B. Johnston, Benjamin S. Flowers, Alan Balfour

SECOND ROW: Richard Dagenhart, Frances Hsu, T. Russell Gentry, Christopher Jarrett, Elizabeth M. Dowling

THIRD ROW: Harris H. Dimitropoulos, Franca Trubiano, Sabir Khan

FOURTH ROW: W. Jude LeBlanc, Michael E. Gamble, Charles F. Rudolph, Thanos Economou, Robert M. Craig, Douglas C. Allen

NOT PICTURED: Libero Andreotti, Godfried Augenbroe, Sonit Bafna, Mario Carpo, Mark Cottle, Ellen Yi-Luen Do, Charles M. Eastman, John Peponis, Gernot Riether, Lars Spuybroek, Perry P.J. Yang, Craig M. Zimring

One Hundred Years from Now: Forming a Vision

Institutions of higher learning gain their distinction and unique authority through the ability to anticipate the need for new knowledge and new tools. In the College of Architecture at Georgia Tech, this need demands an active engagement with man's occupation of the planet and the future condition of the built world.

In this mission, three forces will be formative—the continual growth in world population; the increasing movement of people into cities; and the mounting scarcity of essential resources. Recent trends project that over the next thirty years the world population will rise to eight billion, and two-thirds of these people will live in cities. The majority of such growth and urbanization will take place in the least developed nations—in the weakest economies—and will combine to speed the depletion of essential resources, particularly water and sources of nonrenewable energy.

It is in relation to forces such as these that our College of Architecture must form its vision.

The College, in all its various programs, must prepare graduates to combat the destructive effects due to uncontrolled development and auto-centric realities that cannot survive in a resource-starved world and to commit themselves to tackling the creation of effective and sustainable communities appropriate to all income groups. The way this can be achieved is simple: We must work together. The planners will create the necessary policy and legal framework. The designers will imagine or re-invent the tools of daily life. The architects will organize and harmonize the space in which we live and conduct business. The builders will transform these plans into reality – with energy efficiency governing all. Here I must emphasize that if we did not need to build, we would not need to plan, design, and engineer. But, we must build, and the future needs more building than our current world has ever known.

To this end, the College must seek to promote changes in the building, design, and engineering professions, actively aiming to create a new breed of multidisciplinary professionals. I envision architects, engineers, planners, and builders working together as one, projecting with confidence the impact of their actions fifty to a hundred years into the future and being empowered by digital tools to harness and manage the forces of development in a resource-constrained world. The result would be not only a productive convergence between all the disciplines present in the College but also the creation of new degrees across disciplines, in turn leading eventually to the establishment of professions better able to define and address the challenges of an increasingly complex society.

To prepare for this future, graduates of our programs must have a mastery of the tools and information created by digital technologies. They must utilize these tools to predict the impact of their decisions at every scale on communities and the environment. They must view their knowledge, creativity, and skill as essential and relevant to global as well as local practice. Among these imperatives, graduates must possess a feeling for and the courage to communicate the elegance of ideas in all arenas.

In design, architecture, construction, and planning, future graduates will not be able to adequately contribute to solutions if they do not understand the depth and complexity of global conditions—a knowledge that will only come through meaningful international engagements. Engagement with the world's expanding economies in India and in China must be balanced with studies of the emerging economies in Africa, Central America, and South America. In these places we must combat rapacious resource consumption, uncontrolled population growth, and seemingly irrepressible urban formations of extremes in wealth and poverty. The success of the wealthiest must increasingly contribute to the stability of the rest.

Consider the creation of explicitly humane and public projects committed to applying all the power of our combined fields of knowledge to address planning, design, and architecture in conditions of world poverty.

Consider the scale of the task to be addressed in developing the knowledge and tools necessary to manage and give form to the emergence of global cities—vast concentrations of power, wealth, chaos, and disease. Without the knowledge and vision present in colleges such as this, they will emerge uncontrolled and uncontrollable.

In this year of looking back on our distinguished one-hundred-year history, we must also look to the future and commit all our knowledge, passion, and pleasure in the human condition to forming a better world one hundred years hence.

—Alan Balfour, Dean of the College of Architecture

Francis Palmer Smith

Francis Palmer Smith (1886-1971) received a Bachelor of Science in Architecture from the University of Pennsylvania in 1907 (Phi Kappa Phi; Sigma Xi), and studied under the influential French critic Paul Cret. Upon graduation, Smith was hired as a professor at the newly established Department of Architecture along with George Chapin Robeson, who received a Bachelor of Science in Architecture from the University of Pennsylvania in 1910 and later died suddenly in 1912. Although Preston A. Hopkins was officially the first head of the newly founded degree program, he resigned after only one year and was replaced by Smith in 1909. The academic program of study that he established for the Architecture Program followed the prevailing system in American architectural education derived from the Ecole des Beaux-Arts and additionally influenced by his own education at the University of Pennsylvania. Smith stressed the importance of proportions, historical details, and drawing techniques, all centered on the organization of national competitions. Georgia Tech soon rivaled other design schools in America during his tenure, and the Department of Architecture produced students who laid the groundwork for a strong classical foundation in 1920s architecture.

In addition to teaching, Smith designed campus buildings for the Georgia School of Technology including the Joseph Brown Whitehead Memorial Hospital (1911), the Power Station and Engineering Laboratory (1918), and the John S. Coon Mechanical Engineering Building (1920), and he worked on a proposed Campus Master Plan (1921) designed in concert with Warren P. Laird and Paul Cret. Smith also served as a draftsman for the architect W.T. Downing where he met his future partner, Robert Smith Pringle, in Downing's firm. He served as director of the Department of Architecture until 1922, when he left to form the highly productive firm of Pringle and Smith. Briefly before resigning, Smith attained national recognition for the Department of Architecture by submitting a successful application to the Association of Collegiate Schools of Architecture, the national organization formed to set standards for quality of architectural education for graduates in schools across the nation.

Harold Bush-Brown

Harold Bush-Brown (1888-1983) received both a Bachelor of Arts (1911) and a Master of Architecture (1915) from Harvard University. Before arriving at Georgia Tech in 1922, he was associated with the architectural firms of Jackson and Moreland, and Cram and Ferguson. After the retirement of John Llewelyn Skinner, who served as director from 1922 to 1925, Bush-Brown began the longest term of directorship in the school's history serving as head of the Department of Architecture from 1925 until 1956.

In 1928, Bush-Brown participated in the design of Brittain Dining Hall, the original Ceramics Building, the Guggenheim School of Aeronautics, and several dormitories (Brown, Harris, Cloudman, and Smith). His firm of Bush-Brown, Gailey, and Heffernan was the principal architect for the School of Architecture building, with P. M. Heffernan as the main designer. During the Depression, Bush-Brown took on the position of District Officer for the Historic American Buildings Survey (HABS), which was established in 1933 as one of the New Deal programs to provide employment to architects and draftsmen. In 1936, he worked on the "Outline of the Development of Early American Architecture," a report that examined early American architecture, organized geographically by state.

In 1944, Bush-Brown (and his firm of Bush-Brown and Gailey, Architects, R. L. Aeck and P. M. Heffernan, Associate Architects) became the chief campus architects for Georgia Tech in a design and expansion of the campus plan to absorb the projected increase in enrollment and respond to the technological demands of the day. During Bush-Brown's tenure, the school went through a transition in curriculum and faculty from the Beaux-Arts tradition to the method of functionalist design developed in the German Bauhaus and transferred to Harvard with Walter Gropius. Many faculty hired by Bush-Brown arrived from Harvard at the time when student enrollment increased dramatically after World War II. In 1954, he established a city planning program, then retired two years later as Paul M. Heffernan became director of the School of Architecture in his place (renamed from the Department of Architecture in 1948). In retirement, Bush-Brown wrote *Beaux Arts to Bauhaus and Beyond: An Architect's Perspective* in 1976.

Paul M. Heffernan

left to right: Paul M. Heffernan, William L. Fash, and Harold Bush-Brown (c. 1976)

Paul M. "P. M." Heffernan (1909-1987) began his long-lived and prolific career at the Architectural Engineering Program at Iowa State University, where he earned a Bachelor of Science in 1929. Soon after, he was awarded a fellowship to the Foundation for Architecture and Landscape Architecture, where he won another fellowship, the Condé Nast Fellowship in American Architecture, which included nine months of travel-study. He then returned to Iowa State and earned a master's degree in Architecture Engineering in 1931. He continued his academic studies at Harvard and received a Master of Architecture degree in 1935. While at Harvard, P. M. Heffernan placed first in the 28th Paris Prize, which allowed him to study as an élève (premiere classe) at the Ecole Nationale Supérieure des Beaux-Arts in Paris from 1935 to 1938. Upon his return from Paris in 1938, Heffernan began his teaching career in architecture at Georgia Tech as an associate professor in the School of Architecture, and then he became part of the team of faculty (firm of Bush-Brown and Gailey, later Bush-Brown, Gailey, and Heffernan) responsible for the campus master plan.

His academic and professional honors included membership in Tau Beta Pi, Phi Kappa Phi, Tau Sigma Delta and Sigma Upsilon fraternities, fellowship of the International Institute of Art and Letters in Lindau, Germany, the Royal Society of Arts in London, and the American Institute of Architects (a member in 1945 and a fellow in 1957). Upon the retirement of Harold Bush-Brown in 1956, he was promoted to the position of director of the School of Architecture. The Architecture Program underwent major changes during Heffernan's directorship, including the establishment of a building construction program in 1958, awarding degrees to the first female graduates architecture in 1966, and expansion from a School in the College of Engineering to becoming the College of Architecture in 1975. A six-year curriculum was adopted in 1972, and the fourth-year class was transformed again to become associated with the Ecole des Beaux-Arts in 1975. Heffernan's expansion of the academic scope included not only the Paris Program but also the establishment of a graduate course in architecture, a curriculum in city planning, industrial design, and implementation of research of the built environment, and after 1976, he continued his association with the College as Director Emeritus.

William L. Fash

In 1976, William L. "Bill" Fash (1931-2002) became the first dean of the College of Architecture. Fash came to Georgia Tech from the University of Illinois, where he served as a professor of architecture and director of the graduate program. Prior to his tenure at Illinois, he held teaching positions at the University of Oregon and Oklahoma State University, where he earned his Bachelor of Architecture in 1958 and his Master of Architecture in 1960. He also received a Fulbright Scholarship while at Oklahoma State.

The influence of his leadership was immediately felt with the College of Architecture assuming an intellectual character that placed it on a more equal footing with the larger and more established colleges on campus. Within Fash's first six years as dean, the College celebrated a new building, the addition of a doctoral program, and a growing research agenda by individual faculty that culminated in the creation of major research centers. The Center for Rehabilitation Technology (1980, now the Center for Assistive Technology and Environmental Access) and the Construction Resource Center (1987) became the first two research centers within the College.

In the late 1970s, the College of Architecture initiated a program of study leading to the Doctor of Philosophy degree with a major in Architecture. Through the leadership of John Templer, the doctoral program's first director, the intellectual scope of the College broadened with advanced study, interdisciplinary research, and scholarship in architecture and city planning. In 1982, Georgia Tech and the Board of Regents approved the doctoral degree program in architecture, initiated by Fash.

In addition, Fash implemented an array of research arenas within the professional degree, focusing on building design and performance. As the research program continued to grow in magnitude and capabilities, new proposals were made and grants awarded. As a fairly new branch of the College, the research program was gaining national recognition and esteem as was evidenced by its acceptance of the Human Environment Award in 1982 presented by the American Society of Interior Designers.

Thomas D. Galloway

In 1992, an international search resulted in the appointment of Thomas D. Galloway (1939-2007) as second dean of the College of Architecture, replacing Dean William L. "Bill" Fash who had served in this position since 1976. Galloway's administrative and academic experience included the University of Rhode Island, the University of Kansas, and the College of Design at Iowa State University, where he had served as dean and professor from 1985 to 1992. He received his bachelor's degree in sociology at Westmont College in Santa Barbara, California, in 1962, after which he completed his master's and doctoral degrees in urban planning at the University of Washington in 1969 and 1972.

In the fifteen years of his leadership, Galloway made considerable strides as dean in strengthening the academic and research areas of the College. In addition, he created the Development Council to enrich the academic objectives of the college with expertise and advice from recognized alumni. He was instrumental in securing the P. M. Heffernan House for use by the College for housing the extensive archive of Heffernan's work, as well as housing the retained collection of student work dating back to the first years of the Architecture Program.

In 1999, Galloway initiated the Common First Year, and the creation of two endowed chairs—the Harry West Chair for Quality Growth and Regional Development and the Thomas W. Ventulett, III Distinguished Chair in Architectural Design. The increase in the number of PhD students and the expansion of the programs of study illustrate Galloway's commitment to interdisciplinary education and research, both nationally and internationally.

The key research initiatives spearheaded by Galloway include the establishment of the Center for Geographic Information Systems in 1995; the Advanced Wood Products Laboratory in 2000; and the Center for Quality Growth and Regional Development in 2001. That same year, he reorganized the Center for Rehabilitation Technology into the Center for Assistive Technology and Environmental Access. Under his direction, a number of academic initiatives also were realized, including a new Master of Science in Building Construction and Integrated Facility Management degree in 2001 and a Master of Industrial Design degree in 2002. A Master of Science in Music Technology, Georgia Tech's first academic degree in music, was approved in the fall of 2006. Among Galloway's academic and professional honors, he was named among the "30 Leaders Who Bridge Practice and Education" in America's Best Architecture and Design Schools, published in the 2005 edition of *Design Intelligence*, and as a Lexus Leader of the Arts.

Douglas C. Allen

Douglas C. Allen, ASLA, received his academic training in landscape architecture with a Bachelor's degree from the University of Georgia in 1971 and a Master's degree from Harvard University in 1976. He joined the College of Architecture faculty in 1977 as one of the first hires aimed at expanding the graduate curriculum of the architecture program with its professional two-year Master of Architecture degree. His course History of Urban Form and also his teaching in the College of Architecture's summer program in Italy beginning in 1994 were shaped by his training as a landscape architect. His varied contributions spanning thirty years with the College and the high esteem in which he is regarded by past students and colleagues was made evident by the creation of the annual Douglas C. Allen Lecture named in his honor.

In 2007, Associate Dean and Professor Allen was appointed by then-President G. Wayne Clough to serve as interim dean upon the death of Dean Thomas D. Galloway. During his tenure as dean, Allen was instrumental in securing the resources necessary to successfully compete in the international Solar Decathlon

left: Alan Balfour, right: Douglas C. Allen

competition. Through his direction, the Heffernan Design Archives was relocated to the Georgia Tech Library Archives. He finalized the acquisition of the historic Hinman Building for the College's use. For his longtime stewardship of the College of Architecture buildings, he was awarded the 2008 Governor's Award for Historic Preservation Stewardship by the Historic Preservation Division of the Georgia Department of Natural Resources.

Since 1982, he has been in professional practice, focusing on commercial and institutional projects, multifamily housing projects, residential garden designs, public park designs, comprehensive and master plans, and environmental impact assessments. His practice has been recognized through design awards of excellence including ones from Urban Land Institute, National AIA, Southeast Region AIA, Georgia Chapter of the AIA, and Atlanta Urban Design Commission. Some of his projects include Veterans Memorial Park (with W. Jude LeBlanc) in Smyrna, Georgia (2000-2002); StudioPlex, a mixed-use development in Atlanta (1999-2000); the Augusta Riverfront Center Project in Augusta, Georgia (1990-1992); the Korean War Memorial in Baltimore, Maryland (1987); the development of a master plan for the University of Bir Zeit in West Bank, Israel (1983); the Dash Residence in Atlanta (1996); Piedmont Arbors Condominiums in Atlanta (1986); and the Perdue Garden in Atlanta (1983). He co-authored the book *Cambridge Massachusetts: the Changing of a Landscape* (1979), which won the Conservation Medal from the Victorian Society in America in 1980. He has also published articles "The Code of the City: Window into a Labyrinth" in *Places* Journal 19.2 (2007); "The Park and the Skyline: Monument and Anti-Monument in the Modern City" in *The Conservation of Urban Parks and Squares* (1993); and "The Tanner Fountain" in *Peter Walker: Experiments in Gesture, Seriality, and Flatness* (1991).

Alan Balfour

Following an international search for the replacement of the late Dean Thomas D. Galloway, Alan Balfour became the third dean of the College of Architecture. His tenure as dean commenced in July 2008 and marks his return to Georgia Tech after two decades of administrative service in America and Britain. Educated at Edinburgh and Princeton and also a member of the Royal Institute of British Architects, Balfour has practiced architecture in London and New York, and served on the research staff of the Massachusetts Institute of Technology and the firm of Arthur D. Little.

Following his work as the director of architecture at Georgia Tech from 1978-88, Balfour served as dean of architecture at Rice University in Texas and chairman of the Architecture Association in London from 1991 to 1995. During his tenure as dean of the School of Architecture at Rensselaer Polytechnic Institute from 1995 to 2008, Balfour received the 2000 American Institute of Architects/Association of Collegiate Schools of Architecture (AIA/ACSA) Topaz Medallion for Excellence in Architectural Education, the highest recognition given to a North American architecture educator. This honor was due, in part, to his prolific work as an architectural writer. Augmenting his literature research with studies abroad, in 2002, Balfour spent several months at the American Academy in Rome, which has led to a work in progress on religions and order.

His *World Cities* series explores architecture and urbanism of cities around the world, including *Shanghai* (2002), *New York* (2001), and *Berlin* (1995). For his books *Berlin* and *Berlin: The Politics of Order: 1737–1989* (1990), he received AIA International Book Awards. His recent book *Creating a Scottish Parliament* (2005) links the building's creation with the political structure of devolved Scotland.

APPENDIX B:
RECIPIENTS OF THE PHILIP TRAMMELL SHUTZE ALUMNI AWARD

1981   Philip Trammell Shutze, BS ARCH 1912; Rome Prize, 1915

1982   Julian Hoke Harris, BS ARCH 1928; AIA Fine Arts Medal, 1954

1983   Preston Standish Stevens, Sr., Class of 1919

1984   Paul Malcolm Heffernan, Faculty, 1938-1976; Director, 1956-1975
            Dean, 1975-1976; honorary alumnus; Paris Prize, 1935

1987   Hugh A. Stubbins, BS ARCH 1933

1992   James Harrison "Bill" Finch, BS ARCH 1936

1998   Joseph Newton Smith, III, BS ARCH 1948; B ARCH 1949
            Faculty, 1963-1982; Assistant Director, 1971-1977; Assistant Dean, 1977-1982

1999   Thomas W. Ventulett, III, B ARCH 1957

In the year of our centennial celebration, we are pleased to honor distinguished alumnus and friend
Cecil Alexander, class of 1939, as the 2009 recipient of the Philip Trammell Shutze Alumni Award.

APPENDIX C:
CENTENNIAL ALUMNI LECTURERS

August 27, 2008   John C. Portman, BS ARCH 1950

September 10, 2008   Merrill Elam, B ARCH 1971
and Mack Scogin, B ARCH 1967

September 24, 2008   Anthony Ames, B ARCH 1968

October 15, 2008   Ivenue Love-Stanley, B ARCH 1977
and William J. Stanley III, B ARCH 1972

October 29, 2008   K. Michael Hays, B ARCH 1976

November 5, 2008   Thomas W. Ventulett, III, BS ARCH 1957, B ARCH 1958,
and partners

November 12, 2008   Michael Arad, M ARCH 1999

January 7, 2009   Manuel Cadrecha, BS ARCH 1977, M ARCH 1979

January 21, 2009   The Future of 'The Firm'
Marvin Housworth, B ARCH 1963; Janice Wittschiebe, BS ARCH 1978,
M ARCH 1980; Kevin Cantley, B ARCH 1976, M ARCH 1978;
G. Niles Bolton, B ARCH 1968; William H. Harrison, B ARCH 1971;
Bulent Baydar, BS ARCH 1993, M ARCH 1995; Cannon Reynolds,
BS ARCH 1993, M ARCH 1996; George Heery, B ARCH 1951;
David Goodman, BS ARCH 2004, M ARCH 2006; Susan Lineberry
Baron, M ARCH 1997; Kahlillah Dotson Mosley, M ARCH 2004

February 4, 2009   Harry C. Wolf, III, BS ARCH 1958

February 18, 2009   One Hundred Years of Architectural Education
Elizabeth M. Dowling, B ARCH 1971; Robert M. Craig;
George B. Johnston; Alan Balfour

March 4, 2009   Transforming Urbanism
Brian Leary, BS ARCH 1996, MCP 1998; Ryan A. Gravel, ARCH 1995,
M ARCH/MCP 1999; Steven R. Cover, BS ARCH 1978, M ARCH/
MCP 1981; David Green, BS ARCH 1987, M ARCH 1991;
Edward McKinney, M ARCH/MCP 1996; Bob Begle, M ARCH 1993

March 25, 2009   Libero Andreotti, PhD, BS ARCH 1980, M ARCH 1982

April 1, 2009   Jerome M. Cooper, BS ARCH 1952, B ARCH 1955

Dean; Professor
Alan Balfour

Senior Associate Dean; Professor
Douglas C. Allen, ASLA

Associate Dean; Associate Professor
Sabir Khan, RA

Assistant Dean
Leslie N. Sharp, PhD

Director of Architecture; Associate Professor
Ellen Dunham-Jones, RA, AIA, CNU

Director of Building Construction;
Director of Construction Resource Center; Professor
Roozbeh Kangari, PhD

Director of City and Regional Planning; Professor
Bruce Stiftel, PhD, FAICP

Director of Industrial Design; Professor
Abir Mullick

Director of Music; Professor
Frank Clark, PhD

Director of PhD Studies and Post-Professional Programs; Professor
John Peponis, PhD

Director of Center for Quality Growth and Regional Development;
Harry West Professor
Catherine L. Ross, PhD

Director of Center for Geographic Information Systems; Professor
Steven P. French, PhD, FAICP

Director of IMAGINE Lab; Senior Academic Professional
Anatoliusz "Tolek" Lesniewski, PhD

Director of Center for Music Technology; Associate Professor
Gil Weinberg, PhD

Director of Center for Assistive Technology and Environmental Access;
Associate Professor
Jon Sanford

Director of Advanced Wood Products Laboratory
Karl N. Brohammer

Thomas W. Ventulett III Distinguished Chair in Architectural Design; Professor
Lars Spuybroek

Resident Director of the Paris Program; Professor
Libero Andreotti, PhD

Professors
Mario Carpo, PhD
Robert M. Craig, PhD
Elizabeth Meredith Dowling, PhD
Charles M. Eastman
Nancey Green Leigh, PhD, FAICP
David Sawicki, PhD, FAICP
Stephen Sprigle, PhD, PT
Craig M. Zimring, PhD

Professors of Practice
Brian Bowen
Michael A. Dobbins, FAIA, AICP
David Green, AIA, LEED AP
Harry West

Professors Emeriti
Arnall T. Connell, AICP
Thomas N. Debo, PhD, PE
Rufus R. Hughes II, PhD, FAIA
Larry Keating, PhD, FAICP
John A. Kelly
Ronald B. Lewcock, PhD
H. Randal Roark
Roger F. Rupnow
John A. Templer, PhD

Associate Director of Building Construction; Associate Professor
Linda Thomas-Mobley, PhD, JD

Associate Director of Architecture; Associate Professor
Christopher Jarrett, RA

Coordinator of Master of Science Program; Associate Professor
Godfried Augenbroe

Director of Choral Activities; Associate Professor
Jerry Ulrich, DMA

Associate Professors
Sonit Bafna, PhD
Daniel Castro Lacouture, PhD, PE
Mark Cottle
Richard Dagenhart, RA
Harris H. Dimitropoulos, PhD
William J. Drummond, PhD
Ellen Yi-Luen Do, PhD
Athanassios Economou, PhD
Michael L. Elliott, PhD
Michael E. Gamble, RA

T. Russell Gentry, PhD, PE
Dan Immergluck, PhD
George B. Johnston, PhD, RA
W. Jude LeBlanc, RA
Kathy Roper, CFM, LEED AP, IFMA Fellow
Charles F. Rudolph
Saeid L. Sadri, PhD, RA
Brian Stone, PhD
Perry P. J. Yang, PhD

Assistant Professors
Baabak Ashuri, PhD
W. J. Blane
Ioannis K. Brilakis, PhD
Parag Chordia, PhD
Harley Etienne, PhD
Benjamin S. Flowers, PhD
Jason Freeman, DMA
Frances Hsu, PhD
Javier Irizarry, PhD, PE
Christopher J. Moore
Ronald Mendola
Gernot Riether, DI, Arch.
William H. Russell, AIA
Franca Trubiano, PhD, O.A.Q.
Claudia Winegarden, PhD
Jiawen Yang, PhD

Artist in Residence; Visiting Professor
Ruth Dusseault

Visiting Professor
Philip G. Bryant

Visiting Assistant Professors
Tristan F. Al-Haddad
Donald F. Allen Jr.
Daniel M. Baerlecken
Benjamin J. Diden
Neta Ezer
Kevin D. Shankwiler

*Curriculum Coordinator of
Common First Year; Instructor*
Ann Gerondelis, RA, AIA

Part-Time Assistant Professors
Richard K. Rodgers
William H. Russell

Director of Design Shop
Mercer "Tripp" Edwards, III

Postdoctoral Fellows
Yeon-Suk Jeong, PhD
Ivan Panushev, PhD

Research Scientists
Jason W. Atwood
Danielle M. Ayan
Jason R. Barringer
Karl N. Brohammer
Carrie M. Bruce
Joanie T. Chembars
Amy K. Danner
Jennifer R. Dubose
Sarah A. Endicott
Anthony J. Giarrusso
Alan Harp
Scott A. Haynes
Lisa M. Jackson
Jonathan E. Jowers
Justin L. Kennedy
Lingua Kong
Katherine M. Krueger
Tobias Meyer
Karen L. Milchus
Subrahmanyam Muthukumar
Erik S. Palmquist
Jonathan M. Shaw
Xuan Shi
Ramachandra Sivakumar
Matthew E. Swarts
Traci Swartz
Rob Szurgot
Robert L. Todd
Zhaohua Wang
Graceline R. Williams
Myungie Woo
Hsiang-yu Yang

Staff
Lucie M. André
Leslie A. Bennett
Dracy R. Blackwell
Lisa J. Borello
Beverly J. Brown
Beverly J. Burton
Trent G. Chima
Paul Cook
Catherine R. Denny
Norma S. Denuex
Charlie J. Drummond
Helen L. Emmel
Becky L. Fitzgibbon
Robert Gerhart Jr.
Casey J. Hall
Victoria L. Hall
Frances H. Harris
Karen L. Houston
Patarin W. Intra
Corissa Y. Jones
Lori A. Kishlar
Christopher L. Langston
Jeff S. Langston
Linda L. McBride
Perry L. Minyard
Brenda R. Morris
David L. Morton Jr.
Teresa A. Nagel
Janet M. Peterson
Kerry-Gaye Rainford
Barbara A. Rodgers
Mercedes E. Saghini
Sharon E. Sonenblum
James P. Spencer
Troy J. Whyte
Malina Williams
Lorie Wooten

Architecture Library Staff
Cathy A. Carpenter
Fakhri Haghani
Stephany Atkins Kretchmar
Kevin L. Quick

Lecturers
Edwin E. Akins II
Judy O. Gordon
Frederick M. Pearsall
Stuart M. Ro
Deborah A. Phillips
Joseph M. Ballay
Marc J. Bedarida
Suzanne J. Boyden
Richard Braunstein
Marilyn S. Bright
James F. Butler III
Stephen P. Chininis
Peter Ciaschini
Jamie Cochran
Ryan H. Deaton-Crooks
Lane M. Duncan
Danny E. England
Tim Frank
William E. Garrett
Samuel W. Harris
William J. Jackson
Lee A. Kean
Thomas M. Keel
Jonathan W. Lacrosse
Brian M. Leary
David F. Lynn
Joyce D. Medina
Gary W. Merrow
Michael S. Mesko
Joseph E. Minatta
Craig A. Mitchell
Christopher L. Moulder
Richard L. Porter
Timothy G. Purdy
Soheil Rouhi
Vickram Sami
Raja Y. Schaar
Marco C. Tardio
Dawn M. Trimble
David A. Van Arsdale
Michael D. Watkins
John J. Weitz Jr.
Xavier Wrona
Charles C. Zeagler

IN MEMORIAM
Trent Chima (1958-2009) served the College of Architecture for twenty-five years—first as Director of Shop Operations, then as the early core of the Information Technology Department. His unique kindness and selfless nature truly will be missed.

GEORGIA TECH LIBRARY AND ARCHIVES COLLECTIONS

Georgia Tech Library and Archives, and their digital repository SMARTech. Most of the student work, images, and other historical documentation came from a variety of sources and collections found at the Library and Archives and through their digital repository SMARTech. These include but are not limited to the following:

Blueprint, Georgia Institute of Technology, 1908-2008.

Bulletin, 1908-1968.

Bush-Brown, Harold Photograph Collection.

College of Architecture newsletters, various issues.

Georgia Tech Department of Architecture Annual Reviews, 1911-1931.

Georgia Tech Alumni Magazine, various issues.

Georgia Tech Library and Archives
official website: http://www.library.gatech.edu/archives

Georgia Tech Photograph Collection and Database.

"A Half Century of Architectural Education, Georgia Tech School of Architecture." 1956. A traveling exhibit, in the Heffernan Collection of the Georgia Design Archives, Georgia Tech Library and Archives.

Harris, Julian Photograph Collection.

Heffernan Collection of the Georgia Design Archives, formerly known as the College of Architecture Heffernan Design Archives, which were transferred to the Georgia Tech Library and Archives in 2008.

Miscellaneous Personality Files, including: Anthony Ames, Frank Beckum, Merrill Elam, Julian Harris, John Portman, and Mack Scogin.

"PhD Focus," newsletter of the College of Architecture PhD Program, 2004-2008.

Technique, various issues.

"Thousand Wheels are Set in Motion"
website: http://www.library.gatech.edu/gtbuildings

Whistle, various issues.

COLLEGE OF ARCHITECTURE

College of Architecture Scrapbooks (Volumes I, II, III), compiled by William Fash, Dean of the College of Architecture, 1976-1992.

Various files related to the history and administration of the Architecture Program, the College of Architecture, and the Georgia Tech Architecture Library. On file at the College of Architecture, Georgia Institute of Technology.

PUBLISHED WORKS AND THESES

Bulletin of the Beaux-Arts Institute of Design, various issues between October 1925 and September 1963 (volumes 2-39). Note: The Society of Beaux-Arts Architects founded in 1894 later incorporated as the Beaux-Arts Institute of Design in 1916 and re-established as the National Institute for Architectural Education in 1956.

Bush-Brown, Harold. *Beaux arts to Bauhaus and Beyond: An Architect's Perspective.* New York: Whitney Library of Design, 1976.

Craig, Robert M. *Atlanta Architecture: Art Deco to Modern Classic*, 1929-1959. Gretna, LA: Pelican, 1995.

_____. "Beaux Arts Meets Southern Industry: The Coca-Cola Bottling Plants of Francis Palmer Smith." ARRIS 12 (2001).

_____. "Richard Aeck," "A. Thomas Bradbury," "Burge and Stevens," "FABRAP: Finch, Alexander, Barnes, Rothschild, and Pascal," "George T. Heery," "Ivey and Crook," "Neel Reid," "Francis Palmer Smith," "Stevens and Wilkinson," "Stanley, Love-Stanley," Thompson, Ventulett, Stainback, and Associates (TVS)," "Tucker and Howell," "Emerging Modernism Architecture: Overview," "Modern and Postmodern Architecture: Overview," and "Georgia Institute of Technology College of Architecture." *New Georgia Encyclopedia.* Retrieved 2008-2009: http://www.newgeorgiaencyclopedia.org.

_____. "Two by Ames: Encounters with History and the Modern Aesthetic." ARRIS 17 (2006): 32-52.

Dowling, Elizabeth Meredith. *American Classicist: The Architecture of Philip Trammell Shutze.* New York: Rizzoli Publications International, 1989.

Drury, Warren. "The Architectural Development of Georgia Tech." Master's thesis, Georgia Institute of Technology, 1984.

Fox, Catherine. "Controversy Builds at Architecture Competition," *Atlanta Journal Constitution*, December 9, 1985.

Galloway, Thomas D. and Sara Hart. *Inside/Outside: The Architecture of TVS*. New York: Edizioni Press, 2001.

Griessman, B. Eugene, Sarah Evelyn Jackson, Annibel Jenkins. *Images and Memories: Georgia Tech, 1885-1985*. Atlanta, GA: Georgia Tech Foundation, c.1985.

"History and Verse: An Architect's Poetic Inspiration is Translated by Students into Built Form," *Architecture Magazine*, June 1990.

Ivy, Robert A., Jr. "Preparing Architects to Question and Explore." *Architecture*, August 1988.

Luxemburger, Elaine. "The Transition from the Beaux-Arts Tradition to the Bauhaus Influence in American Architectural Education." Master's thesis, Georgia Institute of Technology, 1986.

McMath, Robert Jr., Ronald H. Bayor, James E. Britain, Lawrence Foster, August W. Giebelhaus, and Germaine M. Reed. *Engineering the New South: Georgia Tech, 1885-1985*. Athens: University of Georgia Press, 1985.

National Institute for Architectural Education, *Winning Designs 1904-1963, Paris Prize in Architecture*. New York, 1964.

_____. *Scholarships, Fellowships, and Awards: National Institute for Architectural Education* yearbook. New York: National Institute for Architectural Education, 1975.

Schwartz, Frederic. *Alan Buchsbaum, Architect & Designer: The Mechanics of Taste*. New York: Monacelli Press, 1996.

Technique, "Accreditation Team Observes Notable Architecture Program," October 3, 1986.

van Leer, Blake. "Faculty-Designed School of Architecture Building, Georgia Institute of Technology." *American School and University*, 1954-1955.

Whistle, "From The Hill," June 29, 1992.

Womersley, Steve, ed. *John Portman and Associates: Selected and Current Works*. Australia: Images Publishing Group, 2002.

ELECTRONIC MATERIAL

American Institute of Architects
http://www.aia.org

Southern GF Company
http://www.southerngf.com

TVS Design
http://tvsa.com

College of Architecture
http://www.coa.gatech.edu

Mack Scogin Merrill Elam Architects
http://www.msmearch.com

John Portman and Associates, Inc.
http://www.portmanusa.com

Stanley Love-Stanley PC
http://www.stanleylove-stanleypc.com

Van Alen Institute
http://www.vanalen.org

INTERVIEWS

Over the course of 2008 and 2009, Elizabeth Meredith Dowling and Lisa Thomason conducted a series of informal interviews, which yielded valuable information about the history of architectural education at Georgia Tech, with a number of alumni, current and former faculty members, and staff. These people include: Cecil Alexander, Douglas C. Allen, Alan Balfour, Kathy Brackney, Cathy Carpenter, Pat Connell, Robert Craig, Richard Dagenhart, Chris Dierks, Lane Duncan, Ellen Dunham-Jones, Barbara Field, John Kelly, Sabir Khan, Ivenue Love-Stanley, Tolek Lesniewski, Robert Rule, Joseph Smith, Bill Stanley, and Franca Trubiano.

Elizabeth Meredith Dowling (left) and Lisa M. Thomason (right)

Elizabeth Meredith Dowling is an architectural historian and, until 2005, a registered architect in Georgia. She received her Bachelor of Architecture from Georgia Tech in 1971, a Master of Architecture from the University of Illinois in 1972 and a PhD in Architecture from the University of Pennsylvania in 1981. Dowling is a tenured Professor who has taught at Georgia Tech's College of Architecture for over 30 years. In addition to teaching courses on Renaissance history and Classical design theory, she developed the College of Architecture Summer Program in Italy and Greece. Currently in its sixteenth year of operation, the program covers the history of art and architecture from Ancient to the Baroque period. She is the principal advisor for the college's Master of Science with an emphasis on Classical Design—the first such degree in the country.

In 2000, she received the Distinguished Faculty Award from the Georgia Tech Women's Leadership Conference and the College of Architecture Faculty Service Award for her leadership efforts to increase the number of women and minority students in the College. In the area of research, she received an International Book Award from the American Institute of Architects and a Bronze Medal from the Georgia AIA for her book *American Classicist: the Architecture of Philip Trammell Shutze* (Rizzoli International Publications,1989). Continued demand for this monograph on the work of Philip Shutze resulted in its reprinting in the Fall of 2001. She received the Arthur Ross Award given by Classical America for contributions to Classical design in the field of education in 2001. She is a member of the board of advisors of the Institute of Classical Architecture & Classical America (ICA & CA) and the current president of the Southeast Chapter of ICA & CA. Her book, *New Classicism: the Rebirth of Traditional Architecture* (Rizzoli International Publications, 2004) is now the subject of a traveling exhibit created in collaboration with Anne Fairfax, principal with Fairfax and Sammons Architects. She has written two additional books on the architectural firm of Harrison Design Associates, Atlanta.

From 2006 to 2008, she served on the Richard Driehaus Prize jury that honors an architect for lifetime achievement in Classical design with a $200,000 prize, and an individual associated with Classical design is honored with the $50,000 Henry Hope Reed Prize. In 2007, she organized the Shutze Design Awards for the SE ICA & CA that sponsors juried design awards in traditional and classical design for architects, landscape architects and interior designers in the Southeastern United States.

Her present research involves currently practicing classical and traditional designers and an associated investigation into the growing interest in all forms of Eclectic design from Gothic churches to Renaissance villas.

Lisa M. Thomason, co-editor of *One Hundred Years of Architectural Education 1908-2008 Georgia Tech*, received her Bachelor of Science in Architecture with Highest Honor from the Georgia Institute of Technology. She continued on as a graduate research assistant and is currently pursuing a Master in Architecture. Together with Professor Elizabeth Dowling, PhD, they designed and curated the centennial exhibit to commemorate the hundred years of architectural education at Georgia Tech, of which is now entirely illustrated in this publication.